THE HUMAN ELEMENTS

Critical Essays

Edited by David Helwig

Introduction

This book begins with the assumption that Canada now has a mature literary culture. There is a constant flow of new work, various in kind and quality, needing neither explanation nor apology. As Robert Fulford has pointed out in a recent *Saturday Night* column, our artists are as important internationally as our politicians – they matter to no-one but us – but most Canadians have begun to accept this as an accident of history rather than as a judgment on our incapacity.

There is an interesting question as to how long the health of Canadian writing, theatre and film would last without government subsidies, but there is no immediate sign that the tap is to be turned off. The process of continuing subsidy is only one way that Canadian society is based on European models, and, as has often been pointed out, subsidies to the arts cost the Canadian taxpayer much less than subsidies to Canadian industries run by believers in free enterprise.

This book has its roots in a weekend seminar on the work of Margaret Laurence held in the fall of 1976. There I found myself articulating my sense that while there was a healthy flow of blood in the body of Canadian literature, criticism was one of its weaker limbs. The critic John Moss was understandably annoyed by my comments, arguing that in my ignorance I was only saying of Canadian criticism what many people had said a few years earlier about Canadian writing.

Though I once made the mistake of agreeing to teach Canadian literature for a couple of years, I prefer to approach it as a common reader. My experience of Canadian critical writing has been occasional. I look at magazines from *Saturday Night* to *Canadian Literature* when they come to hand, and I read critical articles only if I expect to enjoy them.

On the surface then, John Moss was right to suggest that I didn't know what I was talking about. Still, I always remember that the educated opinion of the Jacobean period preferred the plays of John Marston and George Chapman to those of Shakespeare, and this has given me a healthy distrust of educated opinion.

Being the sort of person in whom the itch of argument quickly produces the scratch of activity, I soon found myself at work on this book. If I thought Canaddian criticism a bit weak, let me at least set it to work on the kinds of jobs I thought needed doing. The articles were commissioned from people whose work I knew, and what I told them was that I hoped for essays that would give some sense of creation as a personal adventure.

In the last essay in this book, George Woodcock makes a striking comment in passing. "It needs," he says, "a high degree of cultural certainty to write ... openly autobiographical fiction, and this may explain why in Canada, where colonial inhibitions have weighed heavily upon writers until very recently, it has rarely been done successfully, just as there have been few really satisfactory Canadian autobiographies." In asking writers to read some kind of personal risk and adventure into their subjects, I was hoping to provoke the right kind of seriousness, the kind of "cultural certainty" that knows it is as dangerous to be Al Purdy as it was to be Ernest Hemingway. Only this true seriousness (which must include laughter and has nothing to do with the horrible twins, Pomposity and

Pedantry) allows the poise and urbanity that produces the best critical work.

In the past, I have claimed that there are three fine Canadian critics, George Woodcock, George Woodcock and George Woodcock. Not that only Woodcock has had exciting and seminal ideas about Canadian writing; what I have valued about his work has little to do with whether or not I agree with particular insights. It is the qualities of tone in his writing, the sense that a literate and superbly educated man is engaged in civilized discourse at its most humane, properly aware of both subject and audience, but bemused by neither. I see this urbanity as springing in part from his political sophistication and commitment. The fault of the academic criticism that has always put me off can be seen, in these terms, as a failure of tone, a failure to know the full humanity of its audience, a failure to discriminate just what importance its insights might have for the reader who is also a citizen.

In commissioning the essays for this book, I made no attempt to be systematic or inclusive. The subjects are the accidental products of my discussions with the various writers about what might interest them and help to produce a varied set of essays addressed to the common reader of Canadian books and the common viewer of Canadian theatre and film. My assumption has been that this common reader and common viewer are the same person, and my original intention was to include at least two essays on theatre and two essays on film. I regret that I was unable to make it happen.

I have attempted to publish essays that testify to a personal commitment on the part of the critic. Though my own critical training was under the "new critics" and literary historians of University College, I have usually found the most energetic criticism to spring from some kind of moral stance. Social and political commitment is explicit in Bronwen Wallace's essay on Alice Munro and is implicit in several others. On the other hand, I asked Stan Dragland to contribute because I knew him from the little magazines as one of the brightest and most insightful of formalist critics. I asked Naim Kattan to write about his role as head of the writing section of the Canada Council in order to get a particular and personal view of that important body. Many readers will know, for example, that Canada Council writing awards are decided by juries on which most members are active writers. Kattan's essay gives some sense of the thinking behind that pattern.

Enough introducing. Let the essays speak for themselves.

DAVID HELWIG

Allan King: Film-Maker

Peter Harcourt

I suppose that the stream that runs through most of the
things I respond to is a sense of feeling, of warmth about
people, a celebration of people, a sense of humanity
—Allan King in an interview with Bruce Martin.

W.O. Mitchell's *Who Has Seen the Wind,* published in 1947, is
a loving evocation of the growth of a young boy's consciousness, of his awareness of the cycle of nature and his gradual
recognition of the mystical meaning of life and death. In an
oblique way, a pantheistic way, the novel is deeply religious. It
is concerned with the forces that animate things, both nature
and people. It is aware of the invisible. It acknowledges the
wind.

In 1977, *Who Has Seen the Wind* became a film, adapted by
Patricia Watson and directed by Allan King. One of the
remarkable achievements of the adaptation is that in this most
visual of media they have managed to convey Mitchell's sense
of the invisible by moments of speechlessness. The film is full
of wide-eyed glances, of silent interrogations—as if trying to
come to grips with the significance of things. Largely, of
course, these glances belong to the child, Brian; but they also

are received by both his mother and his father, and they are shared by Digby, the schoolmaster, in the open-eyed trust with which he greets the world.

In this way, the film implies more than it can say. Even the sullen resentment of the Young Ben is conveyed through his body and his eyes. He has almost no lines at all in the film. Admirers of the novel may, in fact, be amazed at how little dialogue has been added. For all of Mitchell's imagery, for all the interpretative function of his prose, Patricia Watson and Allan King have found visual equivalents.

Who Has Seen the Wind is set in the thirties—a world of hard times, of depression and drought. In the last ten years, this has become a fashionable decade for the movies. There have been a number of films that depict that time. But with a difference. In Hollywood films like *Bound for Glory, Thieves Like Us* and *Bonnie & Clyde,* while the *décor* is authentic, the thinking is modern. Especially in *Bonnie & Clyde* which, with its New Deal posters and sense of dusty streets, is the most meticulous of them all, the gestures are totally contemporary. Warren Beattie and Faye Dunaway, while playing characters from the thirties, speak directly to our own times. They appeal to our growing suspicion about the processes of the law and to the value we now place on individual freedom.

In *Who Has Seen the Wind,* there is none of this. With his short hair and clear blue eyes, Thomas Hauff as Digby radiates the idealism that seems so characteristically Canadian – particularly in the past. King used eyes in a similar way in his adaptation for television a couple of years ago of Barry Broadfoot's *Six War Years.* In that play, it was the same idealistic innocence that projected the Hauff character so willingly into the war. In both *Six War Years* and *Who Has Seen the Wind,* Thomas Hauff seems the incarnation of those past times. So it is with everyone in *Who Has Seen the Wind.* There is nothing that seems out-of-period in their gestures or attitudes.

This is both a distinction and, possibly, a limitation. Audiences might find the film too idealistic, too trusting in the natural processes of life to be able to believe that that was how it was in those days. Whether consciously or not, audiences might also be disquieted by its comparative lack of protest. Mitchell's pantheism blurs somewhat the social and political implications of the town's persecution of the Chinese family and of both the Bens. Like the kitten that dies in the litter or the runt pig that ought to be destroyed (as both the novel and the film might seem to be saying), Nature has its rejects as part of its wholeness. While certain characters do protest — principally Digby and Miss Thomson—the whole approach is more philosophical than political, urging us toward mysticism and toward an acceptance of "God's ways."

This idealism in the film, this self-effacing acceptance, is not just fidelity to the original story. There is something of this quality in nearly all of King's work. But in *Who Has Seen the Wind,* Michell's prairie world of the thirties is presented to us with an admirable accuracy. The reconstruction of Arcola where the film was shot (a reconstruction the townspeople were pleased to accept), the circus posters, auction-sale announcements, period gas-pumps, and Bee Hive Corn Syrup cans combine with those trusting faces, with the expressive speechlessness of their eyes, to create within the film a warmly affirmative experience—an experience rare for our times.

The trust and love within the film is largely carried by Brian Painchaud as Brian. It is his consciousness of the world around him that becomes our consciousness of the film. But by a miracle of casting, there is often a sense of tiredness about his eyes—as if in advance of knowing it, he understands that all the questions he asks about life will have no satisfactory answer, as if, finally, the thoughts that most affect him lie too deep for words.

Who Has Seen the Wind is a meditative film. Like the novel it dramatizes, it asks us to contemplate the meaning of human life and the formation of human values. And Eldon Rathburn's musical score assists this contemplation. For those of us who know his work, largely for the National Film Board, many of

13

his devices will sound reassuringly familiar. But they are effective nevertheless. Plucked strings and a Jew's harp help to create the boys' excitement as they prepare for their gopher hunt; and at one point in the film, when Brian walks off into the prairie to spend the night alone under the stars, a solo horn and widely-spaced strings beautifully evoke the landscape's infinite vastness and awesomeness.

Allan King's *Who Has Seen the Wind* goes farther than the book in centring this prairie world within Brian's consciousness. In this way, the film becomes a distinguished example of what is really a Canadian genre: films that create the world through the eyes of a young child. Claude Jutra's *Mon Oncle Antoine* and Francis Mankiewicz's *Le Temps d'une Chasse* immediately spring to mind; but *Lies My Father Told Me* and *Lions for Breakfast* work in much the same way. If we extend the age to take in all the young, then the list of films is enormous – in terms of richness and productivity, virtually the Canadian equivalent of the American Western!

If *Who Has Seen the Wind* is characterized by directness and simplicity, these qualities – which are in the novel and can be found in different ways in other films by Allan King – are finally focused through Brian. Most of the world created for us is presented through his eyes – questioning the values of the life and death around him, trying to make sense of it all but drawing no conclusions. Conclusions (if there are any) would belong to another world, a more urban and sophisticated world – a world closer to our own times.

Certainly, in the past at any rate, it's been very much part of my character to be unsure, to be very careful; it's difficult for me to be very forthright emotionally and even forthright in talking in a general way. I'm not sure how much of it is a desire to be covert or how much of it is a simple confusion in my own head about what I feel or what I think
                                        –Allan King (Martin interview).

14

Who Has Seen the Wind marks a new stage in Allan King's career; for until very recently, King has not been known as a director of dramatic features. Like other Canadian filmmakers, he began in documentary. Working out on the west coast in the late fifties and early sixties, King produced a number of shorts for the CBC that earned him his initial reputation. *Skid Row* (1956), *Rickshaw* (1960), *A Matter of Pride* (1961) and *Bjorn's Inferno* (1964) established the credentials that allowed King to do a variety of items for the CBC, as well as to set up production offices in London, England. It was at about this time, however, that King began to conceive for himself more challenging projects, moving slowly but surely toward a form which he, more than anybody else, is responsible for developing — the actuality drama.

The actuality drama is a mixture of documentary and fiction. By-passing the conventional ingredients of script and actors, it uses actual people in actual situations but then shapes the material so that it becomes both something more and something less than that — a film by Allan King. The purest example of this way of working is *A Married Couple,* made in 1969. But before that there was an interesting predecessor — virtually an invisible predecessor because it has been seen by so few people. It was a film made for the CBC in 1964 called *Running Away Backwards* or *Coming of Age in Ibiza.* In some ways, it is one of the most interesting films that King has ever made.

It is interesting because it is so naive and embarrassing — so uncertain about what its values really are. In this way, it takes risks. *Running Away Backwards* tells the story of a group of Canadians "living it up" in Ibiza — trying to "find themselves" away from the insipidities of day-to-day Canadian life. This ambition in itself is more than a little naive; yet it is an experience that more than a handful of Canadians have felt obliged to go through.

Running Away Backwards offers a dilemma for the spectator.

Is it a naive and embarrassing film about a bunch of Canadians sensitive to the uncertainties of their own identities? Or is it a sensitive and uncertain film about a bunch of naive and embarrassing Canadians who are escaping the demands of maturity by running away to Ibiza? To pose this riddle is to comment on the way Allan King works as a director. The directors we know most about, whom we talk about *as directors*, are generally those that impose a particular vision of the world upon whatever material they handle. Hitchcock, Bergman, Hawks, Antonioni – even Don Shebib – all have a view of life that is developed in one way or another from film to film. They often have as well a recognizable style – or at least a repertoire of stylistic effects that we learn to associate with the work of each director.

With Allan King, however, these matters are most elusive. There have been, to be sure, some thematic preoccupations. From *Skid Row* through *Warrendale* (1967) to *Come on Children* (1973), King has repeatedly concerned himself with social outcasts, with characters who cannot adjust to the conventions that our society lays down as normal. This theme is also present in *Running Away Backwards,* even though these pampered, middle-class people have melodramatically chosen their outcast state.

But more important than theme, perhaps, is King's attitude as a film-maker, which I would characterize as one of self-effacement. Rather than impose himself on his material, Allan King tries as far as possible to let his material speak for itself. Whether it is the immense formality with which he interviews his winos at the time of *Skid Row* or his scrupulous fidelity to the original text in *Who Has Seen the Wind,* as a director King tends to make himself invisible, as if absent from his own films.

One of Allan King's closest affinities could be said to be with Bazin, who believed that it was the cinema's chief privilege to be able to record directly a pre-existing reality. Thus he preferred the extended takes of William Wyler to the subjective

16

camera tricks of Alfred Hitchcock; and he valued the grainy, newsreel quality of the early films of Rossellini over the conceptual editing that has been so much talked about in Eisenstein. I believe, had he lived to see them, Bazin would have also valued the films of Allan King.

Of course, King is not *actually* absent from his own films. But he does stand back in a way, whether through respect or timidity. This is what makes *Running Away Backwards* such a challenging film to deal with. Essentially, it is about discontent – the discontent of over a thousand expatriots who are seeking a "cure" in Ibiza. They are trying to draw strength from a civilization where there is still some harmony between people and their landscape, where there is still a human pace and scale to life. Yet as the old Spaniard explains toward the end of the film, these Canadians are all spectators, unable to understand. "Words which have disappeared from your dictionaries are still meaningful here," as he explains.

Throughout the film, the search is presented as both futile and necessary – as a stage one must go through. There is Jake, who leaves at the end because he has seen the limitations of the histrionic self-assertions that this new world has allowed him; while Hank, who has resisted the idleness and sexual freedom that characterizes this expatriot community, is left behind – supposedly to do some "grad work" on himself with the young blonde who seems both to attract and frighten him, offering a challenge which, at least in those days, Canadians found hard to deal with on their own soil!

Looked at today, the film contains a lot of nonsense. Yet I know it is a kind of nonsense that felt real to many of us of that fifties generation. On a personal, existential level, the film registers a rejection. Yet unlike our existential leaders to the south, unlike Norman Mailer, Ernest Hemingway and Henry Miller, in *Running Away Backwards* he makes no commitment. There is no sense of politics and no concern at all with cultural analysis. They simply spend their time away, "like children playing in a Roman church," as that old Spaniard put it, and then go home again, no doubt to "earn a buck," having dabbled in sex and art.

The film, then, also registers an immaturity – an immaturity which is part of the sense of embarrassment that the film can cause but is also part of its quality. It is as if Allan King and his associates had the initiative to make explicit some of the adolescent over-assertions that certainly were felt by many Canadians of that generation but which few of us would have had the courage to express so openly. In this way, the film documents a certain class of Canadian self-evaders, seeking escape from the monied rat-race but finally so dependant upon it that inevitably they are drawn back. Running away backwards, as the film is called: people aware of an absence, of something their life has denied them, yet only able to affirm it in the most juvenile of ways.

If you have a sensitive, intelligent, quiet, responsive, unobtrusive and unjudging, impersonally critical cameraman or camera crew, then not only is the camera not inhibitive, but it stimulates the [people] to talk, in the same way an analyst or therapist does. You can talk if you want to; you don't have to talk if you don't want to; you do what you want – Allan King in *The New Documentary: a Casebook in Film-Making.*

The same attitudes and problems are present in the next three major films that Allan King directed (in between doing bread-and-butter items, largely from London, for the CBC): *Warrendale* (1967), *A Married Couple* (1969) and *Come on Children* (1973). Each film represents a distinguished example of King's early way of working. They are not "just" documentaries but they are not quite dramatic fiction either; and like *Running Away Backwards,* all three films leave us feeling a bit uneasy at the end.

Both *Warrendale* and *Come on Children* concern themselves directly with adolescents, with young people who have come to feel that they live outside society. *Warrendale* explores the "holding" therapy devised by John Brown for the treatment of emotionally disturbed children – a treatment which (in the film) involves a mixture of extreme caring and something that looks like violence; while *Come on Children* takes a group of "disaffected young people from the suburbs of Toronto" (as the opening title explains it) and sets them up on a farm where they are allowed, perhaps encouraged, to "do their own thing." Of the two films, *Warrendale* is the more disturbing – as much because of the therapy as the film-making. And so, as with other films by Allan King, the experience of watching it leads us away from the film *as a film* and out into a discussion of the material it contains.

Yet the film is not neutral. Nor is the fact of filming in such an environment without its effect upon the kids. Young Tony, especially, who throughout the film is constantly telling everybody to "fuck off!"–a touch of realism that kept the film off the grandmotherly CBC–at one point looks directly at the camera and asks, "Why do I swear all the time?" I don't think it is hard to find an answer. Like other people in the film (though to a lesser degree), he is aware of his "performance."

But the film is remarkable for the environment it creates – both topographical and psychological. The Warrendale clinic looks indeed like a warren of dwellings placed in a mud-and-rubble wasteland – a suburban nightmare which, in itself, couldn't help but increase the sense of isolation that all the children feel. In a way, then, not unlike the attitudinizing adults in *Running Away Backwards,* the kids are cut off from what might be their real culture–from their actual homes in some sort of city dwellings, hopefully more humane than this setting we see them in. While I have neither the space nor the competence to discuss fully the implications of this therapy, it is disturbing to say the least.

I can see its virtues–the virtues of confrontation. The kids are not allowed to retreat into themselves. When they shout or get violent, they are shouted back at in return and held firmly by caring arms. But sometimes this holding involves as many as three adults at a time for just one child. And the kids are expected to verbalize everything. Tony must explain why he resents Terry's bad breath; and Carol must rationalize her resentment of Walter – the fact that she misses him because he is rarely there. Now is this loving force or emotional rape? This is the question that the film leaves unanswered.

The film finds its centre in the death of Dorothy, the cook – one of those "happy accidents" in film-making that allow film-makers to shape their material toward a climax. But even this, considering the nature of the event and the public way it is announced, with all the kids gathered together and the camera ready to roll, is somewhat disturbing.

But as a film, *Warrendale* is important largely because it leaves us with all these problems. It confronts us directly both with the validity of the therapy and with the ethics of film-making. Once again Allan King has taken on a project that many more cautious people would have shied away from.

Come on Children is organized in much the same way, except that there is no "happy accident." One of the girls has a baby, but this isn't dwelt upon; one of the guys shoots up speed. Another lad, John Hamilton, really becomes the "star" of the film. Through his song-writing, he is also a kind of choric commentator. He is constantly playing the guitar and entertaining us with his stories and with all his unfocused charm. A small confrontation occurs in this film when all the parents come up for a day. But even this is low-key – a sad but not basically an angry presentation of the generation gap of which these kids are so aware.

There were a number of films made at the end of the sixties, before the Youth generation gave way to what Tom Wolfe has called the Me generation: Mort Ransen's *Christopher's Movie Matinée* and Jacques Godbout's *Kid Sentiment,* both made in 1968; and Claude Jutra's *Wow!* made the following year. In the context of these films, *Come on Children* is admirable both because of the respect it brings to these kids and because of the quiet rhythm that gradually establishes itself as they sit around and talk and sing and do not much at all. And if the sense of intrusion seems less here than in *Warrendale,* it is nevertheless made explicit at a couple of points in the film. During an early sequence while two of the boys are eating breakfast, one of them becomes increasingly impatient with the fact he is being filmed, an impatience that becomes anger before our eyes. "You're fucking the shit outa me, man," he finally screams, putting his hand up before the camera. And toward the end of the film, as the kids are getting ready to leave, one of them is directly interviewed by King himself—a rare disruption for an Allan King film. "What are you going back to?" we hear King ask from behind the camera; and then a whole series of questions concerning what he is going to do, what he would like to do; if he went away, what he would do there and so on. To each of these questions, in a pleasantly smiling but ultimately hopeless way, the young lad replies "Nothing." Nothing in the world as he has known it. "Maybe get with whatever's happening elsewhere," as he finally puts it.

Like so many of King's films, *Come on Children* presents people without a future, without a culture to sustain them, with no clear idea of what they exist in the world to do. The film starts off with John singing the well-known Dylan song which seems to sum up the feeling of them all:

... I'm walkin' down that lonesome road, Babe,
Where I'm bound I cannot tell....

Miraculously, however, King's discreet direction combines with the editing skills of Arla Saare to give this film in which nothing happens a gently reflective rhythm and distinct shape of its own. It becomes a quiet kind of drama—a drama of nice kids who have a real respect for one another but who feel there is nothing to do and nowhere to go. It's no wonder the film hasn't been seen. It would be too much like an accusation.

Some of the critics ... felt that *A Married Couple* had no imagination or that it was somehow dull. I'm a little puzzled by the expectations for fantasy in film, for myth-making; it seems that if you can give people a comfortable fantasy or myth, it is easier for them to accept. If you say what you feel directly or show them the world as you experience it, this seems to cause difficulties

—Allan King (Martin interview).

Of all the films of this period, *A Married Couple* represents King's most dramatic achievement. However, like most other distinguished Canadian films within this system of ours controlled by American exhibition outlets, it hasn't been a great commercial success. Yet its influence has been considerable, most obviously on the American television series *An American Family* but also on the parliamentary documentation done in Britain by Roger Graef — one of the old team of Allan King Associates when they were based in London.

It is not exactly an *agreeable* film — unless you like to listen to people shouting at one another for the better part of an hour and a half. It is not a film that makes you wish you were married! But what is so extraordinary is that the couple King found to consent to such a project, Billy and Antoinette Edwards, are both natural performers. They bring an energy to everything they do that makes for interesting material on the screen.

Seen nowadays, several years after it was made, the film seems like a study of oppression — largely of the man over the woman but also of all the members of the family by the structure of family life itself. As a family, the Edwards quantify everything. Nearly all their squabbles concern money and the acquisition of material goods — a pair of $40 shoes; a new shag rug; a gas stove for their remodelled kitchen, a washer and dryer, a new hi-fi! Billy, in characteristic fashion, offers the classical male argument: since he makes most of the money, he

22

has most of the rights – an argument that Antoinette strives constantly to counter.

As the Edwards depict it for us, in the edited version of their lives which we have on this film, married life is a struggle for dominance with all the cards stacked in favour of the male. Even their sex-life becomes part of this battle. Antoinette tries desperately to defend her right, when she feels like it, to sleep in her own bed. Talk between the Edwards seems like thrust and counter-thrust, with Antoinette's suggestions becoming more and more preposterous the more aggressively they are resisted by Billy. Like their opening argument about the harpsichord, for example, a scene that reads so tersely in transcript that it seems hard to believe that it never was written:

ANTOINETTE: Where do you think we should put the harpsichord? Over there?
BILLY: The harpsichord. I don't know. The same place we're gonna put the rock band. What harpsichord?
A: That I'm gonna buy.
B: You're not gonna buy a harpsichord.
A: Oh yes I am with part of my money.
B: Oh no, you're not gonna buy a harpsichord.
A: Yes, I'm gonna buy a musical instrument.
B (*shouting*): You're not gonna buy a harpsichord. And the reason you're not buying a harpsichord is because the harpsichord is a selfish instrument just for you. The money is gonna go to buying the things we absolutely need. What do we need a goddam harpsichord for?
A: How can I study voice again if I don't have a musical instrument?
B: You don't need a harpsichord. I'll get you a harmonica.

If there is rarely the sense of a genuine conversation between them, rarely the sense of speech as gentle exchange, the film is not without its moments of tenderness. Billy is often presented playing with their son, Bogart, or fondling their dog, Merton. There is a lovely moment in the film when all four of them are sitting on the floor together, testing out their new hi-fi and exchanging kisses with one another (even with Merton) and listening to that old Beatles recording of "Maria." Right after this scene, Billy and Antoinette are alone together, dancing to "I'd love to turn you on ...," Antoinette all wrapped around Billy as they move together, the image somewhat fractured by the bevelled glass of the French doors that the cameraman, Richard Leiterman, is shooting through. It is a most effective moment, I would argue, because the distance both suggests reticence on the part of the crew concerning this intimacy and, through the splitting up of the image, the scene also creates a pleasant visual effect.

A sadder, more tender moment occurs after a party sequence toward the end of the film. Antoinette has been flirting with some guy in a red shirt which (as the film is fictionalized in the editing) seems to have led to a sort of squabble between the Edwards once they got home. In any case, after the party the film picks them up in close-up, cuddling on the sofa. Antoinette is crying and talking quietly to Billy—possibly the most tender talk in the film. But we can't hear what they are saying. A record they are listening to (one of Sarastro's arias from *The Magic Flute*) erases their speech from the sound-track. Although the scene actually happened this way when they were shooting it, this effect again suggests reticence on the part of the film-makers. It also forces us to deal purely visually with the significance of the scene.

It is not an encouraging moment. Antoinette seems really disturbed, as if trying to reach Billy. But his face is largely turned away from her – as if, as elsewhere in the film, he is rejecting whatever she has to offer him. The scene ends with a dissolve to Antoinette alone in her own bed, cuddling her pillow. Then we cut to Billy, still downstairs, finishing off a drink and patting the dog.

A Married Couple is a highly distinctive film. There is nothing quite like it anywhere in the world. It is a frightening experience. Like the other films of this "documentary" period, *A Married Couple* is also a film about exiles, about people cut off from a culture that might meaningfully sustain them. While there is no political analysis in any of King's films, they all add up to a statement that cries out for political interpretation. They are all about alienation. They present the separation of the individual from culture. Unless we are deeply pessimistic about life and accept all these problems as an unalterable aspect of "human nature," King's films all suggest the need for social change.

Whether King himself is aware of this, I do not know. His characters certainly aren't. Antoinette and Billy see nothing wrong with the institution of marriage as it exists, with their pursuit of the perfect home. The problems are all internalized. Both Billy's dominance and Antoinette's resentment are ritualized in the routines of marriage. At one point during one of their fights, Billy is explicit about this. "The framework isn't the problem," he cries out at her. "The laws of society are not the problem in this marriage. The problem is you and me.... What we don't know is whether we really hate one another or not."

Like both *Warrendale* and *Come on Children,* like most of the early work of Allan King, *A Married Couple* is a film that, in spite of the fine shape that King and Arla Saare finally evolved for it, leads us away from the film as a film, out to talk about the problems it contains – the problem of marriage. And the statement of Billy's could provide a central point from which discussion might begin.

Although the film ends tenderly, it also ends with non-achievement – with Antoinette and Billy seeking the creature comforts of touching one another, of holding one another, but with nothing really resolved. We know that the next day, fresh squabbles will begin. The Edwards are trapped within their own image of themselves: middle-class consumers whose life values are as empty and non-sustaining as the silly Heinz commercials it is Billy's job to supervise. As the film presents them to us, the Edwards' lives are as barren of human sustenance as the wasteland setting of *Warrendale* and as hopeless of a future as the end of *Come on Children*. It is not a comforting picture of our middle-class world.

I'd done most of what I wanted to do in documentary simply as a technical form. I didn't see it shifting very much from there. Also, I had always used documentary essentially as a dramatic form. I've done essay films, but I've always been interested in stories about people. It was never practical in Vancouver where I started to do dramatic work. We didn't have the budgets. We didn't think we had the experience to work in that manner. So one made films about real people and told a story about them.

In essence, the form of *Warrendale* is a dramatic structure; and with *A Married Couple*, it is directly a dramatic structure with two central characters. The fact that they're documentaries, for me, has always been coincidental. That was economically where I could work.

Using actors and scripts has more control in many respects and also allows for a range of experience that is beyond the scope of individuals who are playing themselves. Also, I began to feel that I wanted that kind of control. I wanted to be able to work more directly in a dramatic form, with actors

— Allan King in conversation with Peter Harcourt.

Since the dissolution of his offices in London and of his Toronto company after *Come on Children*, Allan King has been working more than ever with television. But now with a difference. Since 1974, he has increasingly involved himself with drama, involving real scripts and real actors. In some ways this is more conventional work than he has done in the past.

There are several reasons for his switch to drama, both

financial and practical. Financially, in spite of their distinction, King's actuality dramas didn't make much money; and practically, through John Hirsch and the revitalization of television drama at the CBC, all of a sudden work in filmed drama became more of a possibility. There are other factors too that may have influenced him: his increased association with Patricia Watson, now both his colleague and his wife, and his admiration for Toronto's little theatre – for directors like Paul Thompson and Martin Kinch and for playwrights like Carol Bolt, two of whose plays he has filmed.

In fact, his version of *Red Emma* (1976) has much of the old King quality about it. Helped by the constantly steady camera work of Edmund Long, King made what at times looks like a documentary of Kinch's stage production but which at other times seems like a film version of the play itself, with Kinch directing the actors and King his film crew. Kinch worked with King again for Rick Salutin's *Maria* (1976), a film about a young woman in a clothing factory who tries to organize a union. This time, however, Kinch is simply the dialogue coach and King is the director. It is as if, by these means, King has been training himself for the different sort of challenges that dealing with actors entails.

The most innovative of these television programs is *Six War Years* (1975), a video adaptation by Norman Klenman of Barry Broadfoot's oral history of the Second World War. Working directly on tape, King was able to superimpose close-ups in colour of the faces speaking directly to us over black-&-white newsreel footage of the war; and he also had a handful of actors play out a variety of roles. Apparently influenced by Paul Thompson's work with the Theatre Passe Muraille, *Six War Years* might really be described as a piece of "epic" television–a Brechtian combination of direct statement and dramatic re-creation that simultaneously moved and informed us. Its achievement still represents one of the most *original* hours of television that I have seen anywhere in the world.

Less satisfactory, to my mind, is King's direction of

Baptising (1975), drawn from the story by Alice Munro. My own misgivings about this film centre basically on the music. While the story does connect young Del's dreams of romantic love with listening to opera, the decision to run operatic music over her later scenes of love-making has disquieting results. First of all, it gives to all these sequences an Elvira Madiganish sort of lyricism which is a cliché, to say the least. Secondly, the continued use of this music might imply that the *reality* of making love is still wrapped up with Del's dreams. It might suggest that she isn't learning anything, that she isn't growing up. But it is the point of the original story to illustrate the reverse.

Nevertheless, whatever my reservations, *Baptising* too provided a fine experience for its viewers within the opiate world of television. It certainly offered an excellent training ground for the greater challenges of *Who Has Seen the Wind*.

It is difficult at this stage to see where Allan King is going. Since *Who Has Seen the Wind*, King has already made a film version of Carol Bolt's *One Night Stand*, and I assume that he will go on working for the CBC. But he wants to make theatrical features; and even if this means he is working in a more conventional mode, Allan King's artistic presence is still very much there.

The exact nature of this presence is still hard to characterize. It has to do with innocence and also with naiveté – initially about the expected characteristics of the medium he was working in and, throughout his life, about the complexities of existence, especially when seen from a social-political point-of-view. But these twin characteristics are, arguably, what make his films so unmistakeably Canadian, speaking from and to an Anglo-Saxon, middle-class culture which was at one time too dominant but which has become increasingly uncertain of itself since the Second World War. Possibly related to this too is King's lack of self-assertion: in his documentary days, his respect for the reality he was filming; now, in drama, his respect for the original text.

Thinking about King's achievement, I keep remembering Keats' notion of "negative capability" – an openness to experience that Keats believed essential to the receptivity of the artist. This Allan King has in abundance – almost to a fault. Until *Who Has Seen the Wind*, King's major films have all been about rejects, about misfits within the society that contains them. But this subject matter is never analyzed as such. The situations are simply presented to us, always with King's sensitivity and respect; but there is little in the films that might betray King's personal attitude.

Perhaps King's work on *Red Emma* and *Maria* might lead to a more direct awareness of the political issues that form a submerged dimension in all his work. But if his films present characters with no culture to sustain them – culture in the anthropological sense of shared values and conventions – then this might well explain both King's attraction to and the achievement of *Who Has Seen the Wind*.

Who Has Seen the Wind is a re-creation of our past, a past where society was not vitiated by generation gaps and battles between the sexes, a world where – as Helen sings at the beginning of *Red Emma* – "all their lies were true." People believed in things: in the process of Nature, in the continuity of human life, in the necessity of self-sacrifice – as they did as well, more grimly, in *Six War Years*. The male-centred world of middle-class, Anglo-Saxon dominance had not yet been challenged or made aware of its increasing inability to nurture its own children.

Furthermore, the formal tidiness of fiction must be attractive to King at this stage of his career; for fiction provides a stronger sense of order than is possible when working with the raw material of actuality footage, struggling after the event to find an order in the editing. Finally, the extraordinary feeling both of sincerity and wholeness that characterizes every frame of *Who Has Seen the Wind* is all the more impressive because these qualities are the characteristics of a past that still had a strong sense of active community values, values that have virtually vanished from the suburban sprawl of our increasingly urbanized world—the setting of so many of King's previous films.

In this way, *Who Has Seen the Wind* seems to complement Allan King's previous work, as if rounding it off and bringing it to an end. But in its scope, in its newly achieved confidence in working with actors, and in the many extraordinary beauties throughout the length of its fictionalized form, *Who Has Seen the Wind* is also a beginning.

I would like to thank Allan King personally and his secretary, Christine Harris, for arranging for me to re-screen nearly all of these films.

The Literature of Quebec in Revolution

Kathy Mezei

Je crois que l'unité et la "signification" de tout activité résident dans sa complexité et ne peuvent trouver existence, développement et achèvement, en dehors des contradictions inhérentes à la réalité, telle que nous la percevons, la vivons et la transformons dans l'état actuel et changeant de nos connaissances et de nos moyens d'action, telle aussi qu'en grande partie nous la "subissons" sous influence des "forces de la nature" dont nous ne possédons pas encore les "secrets" ni les moyens de les determiner selon une finalité qui serait réellement nôtre

—Pierre Vallières, *Nègres blancs d'Amérique.*

Ce livre est, d'abord l'histoire d'une rupture. Entre des êtres qui s'aiment, bien sûr, mais aussi le récit, par *ce qu'il ne dit pas,* marque une autre rupture: aujourd'hui il est des choses, des événements, des faits, qu'un Canadien français ne veut plus expliquer (il ne s'agit pas de lassitude, mais à force de s'expliquer on oublie de vivre).... L'expression de ces identités nouvelles est encore, forcément, inexacte; c'est pourquoi *Le Couteau sur la table* ne prétend pas être autre chose qu'une approximation littéraire d'une phenonème de réap-

propriation du monde et d'une culture
—Jacques Godbout, *Le Couteau sur la table*.

So closely tied are literature and politics in Québec that certain dates burn like beacons, illuminating the cultural landscape. As Gilles Marcotte has said, "la littérature fait le pays, et le pays fait la littérature." Out of the strands of the feverish political and literary activity of the nineteen-sixties was woven a complex but integrated tapestry of the Québec revolution.

In 1966-67 Pierre Vallières wrote his "autobiography précoce d'un terroriste québécois," *Nègres blancs d'Amérique,* from a New York jail while awaiting extradition to Canada. Out of this search for himself, Vallières tells an eloquent story of a miserable, impoverished, oppressed and tormented childhood, a difficult enlightenment, and an even more difficult commitment.

Hubert Aquin, writer and RIN (Rassemblement pour l'indépendence nationale) organizer, also jailed in 1964 for possession of arms, in his novel, *Prochain épisode,* makes the terrorist and his terrorist acts symbolic of a country and a literary style in revolt.

In *L'Avalée des avalés, Le Nez qui voque* and in *Une Saison dans la vie d'Emmanuel* and *Les Manuscrits de Pauline Archange,* Réjean Ducharme and Marie-Claire Blais present the sadistic yet immensely creative refuge of precocious children described in the "Realm of Childhood" section of *Nègres blancs d'Amérique.* These are diverse sides and diverse expressions of a common québécois experience—oppression by the institutions of church and family, poverty and humiliation, the status of second-class citizens — white niggers — in a wealthy, consumer society, and the fragmentation of a relatively homogeneous society as it undergoes urbanization. In Vallière's words:

... Québec avait l'air d'une ridicule ville de province dont les habitants tournés vers un passé mythifié, s'inventaient de peine et de misère une histoire héroique. Dollard des Ormeaux, Madeleine de Verchères, Radisson....

Novels of the first half of the twentieth century in general either reflected the glorification, entrenchment and encouragement of the rural and traditional values of *"la patrie"* – the fatherland: Louis Hémon's *Maria Chapdelaine* (1914) and Félix-Antoine Savard's *Ménaud, maître-draveur* (1937), or later realistically portrayed the breakdown of these values: Ringuet's *Trente Arpents* (1938), Gabrielle Roy's *Bonheur d'occasion* (1945), Germaine Guèvremont's *Le Survenant* (1945) and Roger Lemelin's novels about the Plouffe family and those who live *au pied de la pente douce*. By the nineteen-fifties a sense of alienation and of vertigo pervaded the culture. Saint-Denys-Garneau had earlier described this sensation of being at rest only in suspension:

Je ne suis pas bien de tout assis sur cette chaise

Et mon pire malaise est un fauteuil où l'on reste
Immanquablement je m'endors et j'y meurs.

Mais laissez-moi traverser le torrent sur les roches
Par bonds quitter cette chose pour celle-là
Je trouve l'équilibre impondérable entre les deux
C'est là sans appui que je me repose
              – *Regards et jeux dans l'espace*, 1937.

This alienation gave vent to a literature of exile, to the existential ennui of Robert Elie's *La Fin des songes* (1950), André Langevin's *Poussière sur la ville* (1953), Gabrielle Roy's *Alexandre Chenevert* (1954), novels in which the heroes faltered and hesitated and despaired, or to the darkening vision of Anne Hébert's *Les Chambres de bois* (1958) and Marie-Claire Blais' *La Belle bête* (1959), which presented the enclosed and grotesque

33

world of the family. So pervasive was the despair and gloom in these authors that the critic Jacques Cotham remarked that the Québécois has devoted all his energy to survival, forgetting that *not dying* is not necessarily *living.*

1960

But in 1960, the Liberal government of Jean Lesage came into power, replacing the corrupt regime of Duplessis' Union Nationale, and the quiet revolution – *la révolution tranquille* – began the long, slow process of laicization, of modernizing education and implementing social measures. Also in 1960, the RIN was founded and the not-so-quiet revolution began to seethe underground. And then, as Hubert Aquin pointed out, "quand tout éclate dans une société, il est peut-être prévisible et même normal que la littérature éclate en même temps et se libère de toute contrainte formelle ou sociale." The literary revolution gathered momentum; André Brochu, writer and *parti priste,* described the sixties as a time when a wonderful deluge of books invaded the long, empty Duplessis night. In Anne Hébert's allegorical poem, *Le Tombeau des rois,* which describes the descent into an underworld of death and an unrelenting past followed by a tentative ascent into the dawn of the future, the falcon, the poet's heart, "J'ai mon coeur au poing. / Comme un faucon aveugle," emerges from the tomb of dead kings and ancestors and turns to the dawn, but with "ses prunelles crevées." It is time to escape from the tombs, values and oppression of ancestors toward a new age, toward "l'âge de la parole" which the poet and painter, Roland Giguère, portrays in a surrealistic sweep of images as a time of difficult but sacred birth:

Un vent ancien arrache nos tréteaux
dans une plaine ajourée renaissent les aurochs
la vie sacrée reprend ses ornements de fer

ses armes blanches ses lames d'or
pour des combats loyaux

le silex dans le roc patiente
et nous n'avons plus de mots
pour nommer ces soleils sanglants

on mangera demain la tête du serpent
le dard et le venin avalés
quel chant nouveau viendra nous charmer?
                                        —*L'âge de la parole.*

For writers like André Brochu looking back at the sixties it was
an age of beginnings and inventions, when Québec literature
benefited from an awakening of the national conscience and
when the people, thrust into a search for their identity, redis-
covered their literature and encouraged their writers as never
before.

There was another event of note in 1960: Jean-Paul
Desbien's *Les Insolences de Frère Untel,* an exposé of the educa-
tional system, was published on 30 August. For the activist,
Desbien's critique on education was perhaps less important
than the attention this priest drew to the question of language,
of *joual*; to speak *joual* is to say *"joual"* instead of *"cheval"*:

> Le 21 octobre 1959, André Laurendeau publiait une *Actual-
> ité* dans *Le Devoir,* où il qualifiait le parler des écoliers
> canadiens-français de "parler joual".... Le mot est odieux et
> la chose est odieuse.

This absence of language — *joual* — is an example of the non-
existence of the French-Canadians:

> ... Nos élèves parlent joual parce qu'ils pensent joual, et ils
> pensent joual parce qu'ils vivent joual, comme tout le

35

monde par ici. Vivre Joual, c'est Rock'n'Roll et hot-dog, party et balade en auto etc.... C'est toute notre civilisation qui est jouale....

One of the crucial weapons of the Québec revolution has, of course, been language: language fought on the fronts of both the literary and political revolution. Among writers and critics, the debate has been endless and bitter whether or not to write in *joual,* whether or not to write in pure Parisian or international French. On the political front one has only to think of the passions aroused not only in Québec but all over Canada as Bills 63, 22, 1 and 101 came before the Québec legislature. Central to the problem of Québec's sovereignty is the question of unilingualism. Attacks against colonialism can be launched by subverting language as well as the institutions of capitalist imperialism. But language in a larger sense than *joual* contributed to the literary revolution. Writers began to experiment with style, tone and with the premises of the "new novel" that had manifested itself in France. As Jacques Cotnam has said, the "explosion" of the Québec novel is echoed in the styles, forms, language and images as well as the themes and aesthetics of the novel. It is difficult to speak of the evolution of the new novel in Québec without succumbing to the rhetoric of revolution and insurrection.

Although the morbid vision and gothic universe of the earlier Anne Hébert and Marie-Claire Blais lingers into the sixties, writers become *engagé* – either in the subversion of institutions, or of language or myths through style. The terrible irony and calm indifference of the first-person narrator in Gérard Bessette's *Le Libraire* throws the bigotry of the church and small town – the Joachines of Saint-Joachin – into humorous perspective through a distancing technique. Sharp social criticism is there, but tinged with dry humour. The old myths that had propped up the Québec theocracy were slowly being destroyed, mocked or inverted by irony (Bessette), satire (Jacques Ferron), black humour (Blais), caricature (Roch

Carrier), realism (Michel Tremblay), violence (Hubert Aquin, Jacques Godbout, Claude Jasmin). To invent *le pays* or *la terre-Québec* as the poet Paul Chamberland called it, required the invention of a new and appropriate language, style and tone. One of the new stylists, Jacques Godbout asks:

> Qu'est-ce donc qui a changé des ouvrages patriotiques du XIXe siècle à ceux d'aujourd'hui? Fondamentalement une seule chose: le style.

1963

In 1963, the terrorist bombings of the FLQ began, the Royal commission on Bilingualism and Biculturalism was set up, and the first issue of the journal *parti pris* appeared. Among the writers and editors of *parti pris* were André Brochu, Pierre Maheu, Jean-Marc Piotte, André Major, Paul Chamberland, Jacques Renaud, Laurent Girouard and Gérald Godin. Those who "took a stand" urged independence, socialization and laicization for Québec; the journal was to pursue a critical and radical description of society. The first editorial outlined these ideals; in contrast to the previous objective and impartial generation, these writers have "pris le parti." They refused the criteria of absolute truth and viewed language – *la parole* – as being an instrument of demystification. The word would help to create a truth that both reflects and transforms the realities of society: "Notre vérité, nous la créerons en créant celle d'un pays et d'un peuple encore incertains." From the personal alienation of the fifties to the *collectivité* of the sixties: the revolution was to occur on all fronts, political and cultural, in the restoration of the uncertain country. The reference to "un pays et un peuple encore incertains" comes from Jacques Ferron's witty *Contes du pays incertain* (1962). The keynote is no longer one of exile, vertigo and despair but one of refusal and affirmation. Out of the group who founded *parti pris* came Les Editions parti pris and the political movement, MLP (Mouvement de libération populaire). Although *parti pris* may be accused of having created a political literature and a literary politics, that journal and the publishing house Hexagone, started by the poet Gaston Miron, played an important role in circulating revolutionary ideas among the public, and in inspiring and educating people. Moreover, *parti pris* also explored the question of *joual*. Jacques Renaud's novel *Le Cassé*, the first written in joual, published by Les Editions parti pris in 1964, caused an uproar. Renaud's reprisal in *parti pris* was vehement:

> Vous voulez avoir mon avis? Le joual, c'est, je crois, alternativement, une langue de soumission, de révolte, de douleur. Parfois les trois constantes se mêlent et ça donne un bon ragoût.... Je n'arrive pas à me revolter dans la langue de Camus.... Ma révolte est celle d'un canadien-francais, ses mots et ses tournurnes de phrases sont canadiens-français, plus spécifiquement montréalais, jouaux
> —XI. 22, janvier 1965.

Or as Gérald Godin put it: good French is the desired future of Québec, joual is its present.

1965

The preliminary report of the Commission on Bilingualism and Biculturalism discovered that "the idea of a French-Canadian nation, having a common language, territory, history, and a common culture or way of life was expressed by many people who have no association with separatism."

The White Paper on the Constitution presented the Fulton-Favreau formula which was not in favour of Québec's attaining special status. The terrorist bombings had also inspired a stronger and more violent form and subject in the literature. It was a good year for novels. As Claud Jasmin (RIN worker and FRAP candidate in Montréal) wrote in the English translation of *Ethel et le terroriste*:

The writing of this book is one manifestation of the acute examination of conscience which seized French Canada in the spring of 1963 ... [we were] rudely shaken when a terrorist bomb ... [killed] the night watchman Wilfred O'Neil (he of the Irish surname and French tongue). "We felt it our duty as writers to enlighten the people."

Both Godbout's *Le Couteau sur la table* (1965) and *Ethel et le terroriste* (1964) and, in a sense, Aquin's *Prochain épisode* (1965) are a response to the death of the night watchman. All three novels take as their hero or anti-hero, a terrorist who has or is about to set off a bomb or commit a violent act. Since Malraux's *La Condition humaine* and Sartre's *Le Mur,* the terrorist has been the existentialist hero *par excellence,* torn by the choice between life and death, action and non-action, a Hamlet figure, as Aquin suggests, with a deadly hesitation before the desire and the inability to act. These three terrorist novels, written in the first person, pursue several themes that become endemic to the revolution of the sixties, themes about the difficulty of loving, the desire to create (or recreate) one's country, *pays, terre,* the role and nature of revolution, the insidious encroachment of American culture and in *Prochain épisode,* the process of writing.

In *Prochain épisode,* the act of making love, starting revolutions and inventing one's country are fused with the agony of writing:

Je t'écris infiniment et j'invente sans cesse le cantique que j'ai lu dans tes yeux; par mes mots, je pose mes lèvres sur la chair brûlante de mon pays et je t'aime désespérément comme au jour de notre première communion.

39

In *Ethel et le terroriste,* the hero, Paul, flees from Montréal to New York with his Jewish girlfriend in a ten-year-old shit-yellow jalopy after setting the bomb he later learns has killed a man. The physical movement from remembered or imagined place to place provides a framework for the movement through the narrator's mind and for a discovery of his homeland. The voyage undertaken by the narrator of *Le Couteau sur la table* and his girlfriend, Patricia, performs the same symbolic function, and the litany of dates and places in *Prochain épisode* – 24 June, St.-Jean Baptiste day, the Rebellion of 1837, and St.-Eustache where the *patriotes* were defeated – is also an attempt to create a history for *le pays.*

In these three novels the association between the women who are the lovers of the narrators and *Terre-Québec* is a striking recurrence. Presented as rather flat and stereotyped characters, the women become symbolic anima figures. Patricia and Madeleine, who complete the *ménage à trois* in *Le Couteau sur la table,* are polarized aspects of Québec – the wealthy Anglo-Saxon, indifferent to the political issues and addicted to a tinsel culture, and the oppressed but vital east-side *québécoise* who dies an untimely death. In turn, Patricia, object of love and hate, will become the object of the narrator's violence when he can no longer tolerate his dependency on her. And Ethel comes from a race at least as persecuted as the *québécois.* The hero of the spy intrigue written by the narrator in *Prochain épisode* is smitten with an elusive K (Kébec?) who is possibly a double agent. Again the relationship with one's *pays* is ambivalent. The song of the land which becomes the song of woman is a theme that weaves through the poems of Roland Giguère, Paul Chamberland, Gaston Miron, as they also seek to invent and find a homeland.

The structures of *Le Couteau sur la table* and *Prochain épisode* are much more complex than that of *Ethel et le terroriste* though all three blur distinctions of time and space, and present flowing and impressionistic interior monologues. In *Prochain épisode,* the jailed terrorist is writing a spy novel. The form of

Aquin's *Trou de mémoire* (a detective novel based on *"pharmaco-manie"*) and *L'Antiphonaire* is also organized around a pursuit. The intrigue is an effective form for verbal plays and narrator-reader-author games and *double entendres*. Because the narrator-subject is pursuing an object, a dialectic is set up between two forces. The detective or pursuer or terrorist, like the narrator and reader, is an investigator of facts, of clues which he attempts to piece together in order to find or discover or invent his object. Detection becomes a metaphor of the process of reading. As Pierre Turgeon said in his detective novel, *Prochainement sur cet écran,* the objects pursued are

> de pures créations de notre esprit et, avec le temps, ils nous ressemblent de plus en plus. De sorte que dans le genre d'enquête on finit toujours par se poursuivre soi-même.

The hero of the spy intrigue in *Prochain épisode* finds that the object of his pursuit, the mysterious M. de Heutz, has strangely similar tastes in art, furniture, good food, wine and women and spins the same fantastic yarn as the hero, to save his skin. Is the blonde K beloved by the hero the same blonde he glimpses with de Heutz? With the distinctions between the hero and de Heutz blurred as well as between narrator and hero, is it possible that the pursuer and the pursued are one?

It is in *Prochain épisode* that the analogy and affinity between political and literary activity are most clearly presented. But terrorism or other forms of political action become, for so many *québécois* writers of the sixties, the most appropriate form within which to describe their *"condition humaine."* According to Aquin—and this is essentially the premise behind the *parti pristes*—the writer is obliged to be politically *engagé*. But, as the hesitant narrator-writer of *Prochain épisode* demonstrates, it is difficult to write in a dominated country: the writer-revolutionary breaks with the coherence of domination and begins a Hamlet-like monologue interrupted at each word. "Mon récit est interrompu, parce que je ne connais pas le premier mot du prochain episode." The revolutionary writer's role is to be a terrorist of style. "Tous les mots de la suite me prendront à la gorge; l'antique sérénité de notre langue éclatera sous le choc du récit ... des sigles révolutionnaires seront peinturés au fusil à longueur de pages.... Les pages s'écriront d'elles-mêmes à la mitraillette: les mots siffleront au-dessous de nos têtes, les phrases se fracasseront dans l'air...." This "subversive" style: monologues, interruptions, flashbacks, staccato shots and retorts, violence to pure French and to syntax, compression and distortion of linear narrative, surrealistic juxtaposition of time and space, past and present permeate the work of the writers of the sixties.

Also in 1965 Marie-Claire Blais' most famous novel, *Une Saison dans la vie d'Emmanuel,* appeared, drawing together all the obsessions of Québec. Nothing remained sacrosanct – Church, family, rural life – in this novel which clothed the miseries and hypocrisies of the French-Canadian family in black humour and mordant caricature. Jean Le-Maigre, the youthful hero and narrator, is also a chronicler of this life of desperation, this life that is a short, bitter, winter season, as he lies dying of tuberculosis. The first-person child narrator-author appears frequently in the novels of Marie-Claire Blais, in the volumes of *Les Manuscrits de Pauline Archange* as well as in Ducharme's *Le Nez qui voque,* constructing his own imaginary world against the horrors of the present. (The child's voice and vision is a common occurence in Québec fiction, as in Ducharme's *L'Avalée des avalés,* Blais' *La Belle bete,* Hébert's *Le Torrent* and *Les Enfants du sabbat,* André Langevin's *Une Chaîne dans le parc* and Jacques Ferron's *L'Amélanchier,* and may represent a necessary first stage in the development of a mythology and tradition in Québec.) But, as in *Prochain episode,* the act of writing, if not necessarily a politically revolutionary act, is a rebellion, an assertion, a desperate fight for life.

What distresses Pauline in *Les Manuscrits de Pauline Archange* is the thought that while it is so difficult for her to live, "dans un livre, cela ne prendrait que quelques pages, et que sans ces quelques pages, je risquais de n'avoir existé pour personne." The narrator-authors who emerge in the novels of Gérard Bessette (*Le Libraire*) or Aquin (*Prochain episode, Trou de mémoire, L'Antiphonaire*) or Réjean Ducharme (*Le Nez qui voque*) are scarcely prototypes of young Stephen Daedalus setting out to forge the uncreated conscience of his race. On the contrary, the "je" of many novels insists upon the absolute necessity of writing in order to fend off death:

Le roman que j'écris, ce livre quotidien que je poursuis déja avec plus d'aise, j'y vois un autre sens que la nouveauté percutante de son format final. Je suis ce livre d'heure en heure au jour le jour; et pas plus que je ne me suicide, je n'ai tendance à y renoncer   —*Prochain episode.*

or madness:

Je viens de commencer un roman infinitesimal et stricte-ment autobiographique.... Le roman d'ailleurs c'est moi: je me trouble, je me décris, je me vois, je vais me raconter sous toutes les coutures, car, il faut bien l'avouer, j'ai tendance à déborder comme un calice trop plein   —*Trou de mémoire.*

or fear:

Je rédige cette chronique pour les hommes comme ils écri-vent des lettres à leur fiancée. Je leur écris parce que je ne peux pas leur parler, parce que j'ai peur de m'approcher d'eux pour leur parler.... J'écris mal et je suis assez vulgaire   —*Le Nez qui voque.*

or boredom:

Tous ces détails, je m'en rends compte, n'offrent aucun intérêt. Peu importe. Autant d'écrit, autant de pris. Ça passe le temps. Et ce que ça peut être long un dimanche!...

Alors je redige ce journal.... Pourvu que ça continue; que je
trouve quelque chose à dire   —*Le Libraire.*

These problems of the writer in bringing forth his creations
parallel the difficult and painful birth-pangs of a nation on the
verge of creating and inventing itself. Another problem con-
fronting the colonized writer is the language of his novel. Since
one's language reflects one's condition it may be imperative to
write in *joual*. Michèle Lalonde's renowned poem *Speak White* is
a monument to the condition and the language:

Nous sommes un peuple inculte et bègue
mais ne sommes pas sourds au génie d'une langue
parlez avec l'accent de Milton et Byron et Shelley et Keats
speak white
et pardonnez-nous de n'avoir pour réponse que
les chants rauques de nos ancêtres et le
chagrin de Nelligan....

But language can be in revolt in ways other than *joual* by
distorting syntax and inventing words. In Ducharme's *L'Avalée
des avalés,* Bérénice describes how she goes to the market-place
and shouts in *bérénicien*:

Je me rends sur la place du marché et là je parle à tue-tête en
bérénicien. Tout ce que j'ai dit jusqu'ici est demeuré
infécond.

In *Le Nez qui voque,* the narrator introduces himself in a series of
puns:

Ils ont des tâches historiques. Sans accent circonflexe, nous
obtiendrons: ils ont des taches historiques. C'est une équivoque. C'est un nez qui voque. Mon nez voque. Je suis un nez
que voque. Mon cher nom est Mille Milles. Je trouve que
c'est mieux que Mille Kilomètres.

44

1968

By the late sixties both political and literary revolutions were firmly set in motion. A group of writers and musicians toured the universities with their "Poèmes et chants de la résistance" to raise money for the imprisoned Pierre Vallières and Charles Gagnon. The Parti québécoise was created out of the Mouvement Souverainté-Association; its leader was René Levesque. The success of Michel Tremblay's play, *Les Belles-Soeurs,* indicated an acceptance of *joual* as a literary medium, and of the ability of the *québécois* to confront his image with some measure of humour. The publication of Roch Carrier's *La Guerre, Yes Sir* initiated a trilogy that took a humorous if sardonic look at rural customs and values presented in a colourful montage. Certain recurring preoccupations of *québécois* writers were being woven into new and more enduring forms. The sixties were a time of refusal and of invention. Taking to heart the 1948 manifesto, *Refus global,* of the automatistes, Paul-Emile Borduas and Claude Gauvreau, which "refused" the oppressions of a rigid conservative theocracy and cried "yes" to the marvellous, the miraculous and to life itself, the writers of the sixties, those who were politicized – Aquin, Chamberland, Jasmin – and those who were not – Hébert, Bessette – refused or inverted the old myths and invented new ones. As Anne Hébert claimed in 1960: "Notre pays est à l'âge des premiers jours du monde. La vie ici est à découvrir et à nommer...."

1970

La Nuit de la Poésie took place on Good Friday in a Montréal theatre where poets read their works throughout the night. But, in October, the participants in the Québec literary and political revolution received a shock which even the unexpected PQ victory in 1976 has only begun to mitigate. The events of October 1970 – the kidnapping of James Cross and Pierre Laporte, the implementation of the War Measures Act, the murder of Laporte and the detainment of hundreds of *québécois* deprived of their civil rights—were not easily forgotten or absorbed by the literary imagination. Québec entered what André Brochu called the purgatory of 1970 to 1976.

Consequently Victor-Lévy Beaulieu, prolific novelist and essayist, complained in *Le Devoir* that Québec is a *"pays équivoque"* (est-ce que c'est son nez qui voque?):

> Le pays équivoque constituait votre force parce qu'il flottait dans le non-espace, faisant de vous un médium, capable de tout, même de ne pas être et pourtant d'y être parce que justement on n'y était pas (2 October, 1976).

He claimed that although Québec is searching for a place and a direction she ends up looking only at her own image; instead of using myths, the writers chase the myth of their selves, substituting chronicles and episodic tales for the epic. The epic of Québec remains to be written. And it is strange that it has not yet risen out of the ashes of the October Crisis.

While the terrorist novel, the blatant political metaphor, no longer dominates, the terrorism of style continues—*joual* has infiltrated many of the novels and plays. In fact, Marie-Claire Blais and Jacques Godbout weave amusing tales around the relationship between the writer and *joual*. Partly as a response to criticisms of her lack of grounding in the contemporary realities of Québec, Blais wrote *Un Joualonais, sa joualonie* (1973). In this "chronicle," the abused, rootless orphan Ti-Pit, whose real name is, ironically, Abraham Lemieux (Abraham: the father of our people and Lemieux: the best), becomes the unwilling protégé of the poet Papillon. Papillon wants to vitalize his poetry and asks Ti-Pit to teach him his language "joualon."

> Tu sais une chose, Lemieux? Je suis amoureux de ta langue, j'en suis épris, il y a longtemps que je me penche sur les

46

mots, le verbe est mon culte, tu m'écoutes ou tu m'écoutes pas, Sacrament?
Je vous écoute.
Tu me dis "tu," tout de même! Je suis pas un trou-de-cul, comme on dit en joualon. Tu sais ce que je veux dire, le joualon, ta langue?
Ouais. J'avais compris. Mais pourquoi que vous me parlez à moé, j'suis pas un intéressant!
Abraham, t'as des choses à me dire....

In *D'Amour, PQ* (1972) Jacques Godbout pokes similar fun at another writer with inflated rhetoric, Thomas D'Amour. Appropriately, Godbout dedicates his book to Raoul Luoar Yaugud Duguay, poet and Monsieur Toulmonde, in these words: "à un moment donné TOULMONDE est demandé au parloir."

As Mireille, the down-to-earth and earthy secretary types D'Amour's "poetic" manuscript, she falls in love with the author, though in despair with his style and subject. Fed up with his pompous language, she exclaims:

Thomas D'Amour et ceux de sa caste me donnent envie de crucifier l'imparfait du subjonctif. Dès qu'ils ouvrent la bouche, comme une fenêtre trop grand, je voudrais leur fourrer au fond de la gorge un mot juteux, un mot mouche, justement, un mot de rue, un mot bon, pas un bon mot, un mot au fenouil, un mot scotch, un mot poivré comme j'aime les Bloody Mary, un char de mots dans la gorge douze par bancs, puants, parfaits.

Together, Mireille and Thomas write instead, in bed, a detective story! And the last word is Mireille's: "Un écrivain, c'est pas plus important qu'une secrétaire, oké?"
Another seventies solution to the problem of the terrorist-intrigue novel has been Claude Jasmin's *Revoir Ethel* (1976), a

sequel to *Ethel et le terroriste*. Paul, emerging from jail as "Germain," sets out across America, this time in an old red '67 Camaro, with two strange companions, in search of his grand passion – Ethel. FLQ becomes, as Paul Chamberland once quipped, Faire L'Amour Québécois. The fascination-repulsion with American culture, a persistent note in Jasmin's novel, emerges as a dominant preoccupation of the recent fiction; it marks Victor-Lévy Beaulieu's work: *O Miami, Miami, Miami* (1973) and *Jack Kérouac: essai-poulet* (1972) and Ducharme's *L'Hiver de force* (1973), an exposé of the vacuous lives of André and Nicole (not his usual children of charm by the way, but, this time, arrested adults) befuddled by television, beer and fast foods.

Writers also begin to discover a wealth of anecdote and event in Québec's heritage or *patrimoine*. In his *Manuel de la petite littérature du Québec*, Levy Beaulieu reaches back into historic memory to expose the sordid religious tracts, the gruesome lives of martyrs that constituted the popular or *petite littérature* of the nineteenth and early twentieth century, something he feels has haunted the *québécois* imagination. His novel, *Les Grand-pères* (1971), a fictional version of the *petite littérature* of *petits hommes* is a burlesque, a grotesque slice of the sordid life of an old peasant.

Interest in unusual events in Québec's past also prompted Anne Hébert to reach back into the nineteenth century for a tale of intrigue, a love triangle and murder. *Kamouraska* (1970) becomes a poetic and symbolic entry into the mysteries of the romanticized past of the heroine, Elizabeth, and of a dying seigneurial tradition. It is also, an affirmation of passion and love over death and duty.

In Jacques Ferron's *Le Saint-Elias* (1972), set in the early nineteenth century, the villagers' lives, which revolve around the trading barque, the *Saint-Elias*, the village's contact with the wider world, are described ironically and whimsically by the master portrayer of the uncertain country. In *Les Enfants du sabbat* (1975), Anne Hébert enters the realm of black magic:

the black sabbath. *Les Enfants du sabbat* presents a world in which the Church is not only exposed for its hypocrisy and ignorance (as in *Une Saison dans la vie d'Emmanuel* or *La Guerre, Yes Sir*), but is superseded by a greater magic – the magic of evil.

As Québec culture in the seventies moved toward unilingualism and a cultural if not political independence, the political metaphors of the sixties are shed in favour of other modes of explicating and revolutionizing the culture and heritage. The feminine consciousness, for one, has been slowly given voice and experimental form in the works of Nicole Brossard, Louky Bersianik, Monique Basco and Hélène Ouvard. The new generation of writers also wants a *patrie,* but Jacques Godbout suggests that in order for it to exist, Québec needs a *patrimoine* or heritage. Consequently the literary *patrimoine* requires a fount of patriotic works. But this call for "patriotic works" is not the propaganda of the poets of *L'Ecole patriotique* of the eighteen-sixties or of the *Terroir* writers of the early part of this century or even of the *parti pristes* of the sixties. From Anne Hébert's macabre and exotic treatment of the Catholic heritage in *Les Enfants du sabbat* to Lévy Beaulieu's burlesque of peasant life and Blais' parody of the female libbers, prostitutes and naive worker-priests who populate *La Joualonie,* to Roch Carrier's satire on urban development in *Le Deux-Millième etage* (1973), Ducharme's parody on urban *joualonie* life in *L'Hiver de force,* to the fantasy, nightmare forest world of Carrier's *Floralie, où es tu* (1969) and Jacques Benoît's *Jos Carbone* (1967), the tapestry formerly pieced together by nationalist fervour has expanded into a wider and deeper exploration of the *patrimoine.*

15 November 1976

With the victory of the Parti québécois on a platform of *souveraineté-association,* the newspapers announced: the poets are in power. Gérald Godin, poet, *parti priste,* had won the riding of Mercier, defeating Robert Bourassa. Michel Tremblay, en

49

route to Paris in despair over Québec's stagnation, hearing of the PQ victory, promptly returned home. But the victory of the Parti québécois poses some interesting questions for the *engagé* writers and artists. What will be the repercussions for the artists of this *political* victory? What of apolitical writers like Anne Hébert – what is their place in a literary clique that demands political commitment? Will the writers participate in the *collectivité* or continue to turn inward and to the past or will they abandon the pen for the political arena? Even if independence seems "possible," what of the social revolution? What will be the relationship between the government and the artist? Both the Green and forthcoming White Papers of the former Minister of Cultural Affairs, Jean-Paul L'Allier and of the present Minister, Louis O'Neill, are attempts to deal with the role of the government in the arts. And most crucial of all, the finest hour having arrived, will the artists lose their fervour? In an 1977 issue of *Liberté,* entitled *"divergences"* (a reference to Jean Le Moyne's critical essays on Québec society and culture, *Convergences,* 1961), the editors, troubled by these questions, examine the direction and vitality of Québec literature and compare the militant writer of 1965, the "guerrier" who played a vital role in the collective life, with the writer of today who is more isolated, more turned in upon himself. And Lévy Beaulieu, reflecting on the consequences of November 15, complained that Québec fiction, instead of following the movement that brought the PQ to power, has borrowed other "voices" that express a colonial situation – the voices of dispossession, schizophrenia, mutilation and death. Are the writers of the seventies beginning to repeat themselves, mulling over the same issues, examining the same landscapes and villages, the same stereotypes, the same *"mouvement joualisant et petite culture"?* Is the small nation of Québec becoming closed in on itself, unenlightened by reciprocal exchanges with other cultures? Are writers participating in an incestuous circle of exaggerated praise and interchange? It seems that the struggle of the writer between his role as a voice for the *collectivité* and as a voice of his own personal necessity, salvation and vision continues, and that the developing independence of Québec culture has certain drawbacks.

15 March 1977

In the gardens of Ville-Marie Collège, Hubert Aquin, perhaps Québec's finest novelist and intellect, shot himself. He left he following note.

Aujourd'hui 15 mars 1977, je n'ai plus aucune réserve en moi. Je me sens détruit. Je n'arrive pas à me reconstruire et je ne veux plus me reconstruire. C'est un choix. Je me sense paisable, mon acte est positif, c'est l'act d'un vivant. N'oublie pas en plus que j'ai toujours su que c'est moi qui choisirai le moment, ma vie a atteint son terme. J'ai vécu intensement; c'en est fini.

A gesture of personal despair? A warning? A promise?

Women's Lives: Alice Munro

Bronwen Wallace

There is a change coming I think in the lives of girls and women. Yes. But it is up to us to make it come. All women have had up till now has been their connection with men. All they have had.

After my first reading of *Lives of Girls and Women,* passages like this one stayed with me. I wrote them on the note-board above my desk, quoted them endlessly to my friends. I think I saw the book as a kind of female answer to *Catcher in the Rye* – and Canadian as well. The information gained from the few articles (mainly in women's magazines) I read on Alice Munro merely strengthened my impression. Here was a woman from a small Ontario town, who married young, had three children (all girls!) and still managed to find time to write. Her first collection, *Dance of the Happy Shades,* won the Governor General's Award in 1968 and her first novel became a bestseller. In interviews she talked honestly and openly about her experience as a woman and about her feelings toward the women's movement.

My admiration increased with the publication, in 1974, of her second collection of short stories, *Something I've Been Mean-*

ing to Tell You. By that time I myself had had a child and had begun to write more seriously. And here were stories that handled the complicated themes of mother-child relationships and the whole question of women writers in ways that I could recognize. Again I was impressed by the intensity with which the perceptions of the women characters were presented, the power of the images used to convey these perceptions. As well, I was more acutely aware of the *range* of characters. The collection included stories in which the centre of consciousness was, variously, that of a housewife, an elderly man, an elderly woman, a teenage girl. There were stories written from the perspective of middle-class women as well as women who had worked as maids. And although I still responded most strongly to those characters whose experience was most like my own, I could appreciate Munro's ability to bring an equal intensity to such a diversity of perceptions.

All of which brings me to this essay and the context in which it is written. It is written from a feminist perspective in the sense that it explores primarily the way in which Munro presents the experiences and perceptions of women; it recognizes that her writing is powerfully centred in her understanding of her own experience as a woman.

This does not mean that I see Alice Munro as a writer of "manifesto" novels or stories in the way that, say, Marge Piercy (*Small Changes*) is. I think such fiction is often valuable, but, although Munro may deal with similar themes and situations, she does so, I think, from a different point of view. Her work, I believe, recognizes that the perceptions of women, the way women order their lives is not only very different from the way men order and experience theirs, but also powerful because of those differences, because of their situation as women.

In an interview with Kem Murch in *Chatelaine* (May, 1974) Alice Munro said: "A subject race has a kind of clarity of vision and I feel that women have always had a clarity of vision which men were denied. And, in a way, this is a gift, it goes along with a lack of power. And I valued that very much—the value of being able to see clearly." Such a statement contains many powerful implications and I see Munro's work as an exploration of many of them. The form she has chosen, the short story, is admirably suited to these explorations because of its flexibility, its capacity to sustain intense perceptions. And I think it is her facility with the form as well as her clarity of vision that has allowed her to explore such a wide range of perceptions – including, occasionally, those of men – and to understand the strengths and limitations of each.

We drove through country we did not know we loved – not rolling or flat, but broken, no recognizable rhythm to it; low hills, hollows full of brush, swamp and bush and fields.

For me, the power of Munro's work emerges first from its centre in the flat, solid reality of things. Behind everything she writes, the particular physical landscape is simply there. It is of course often imbued with human emotions, as it is for example during Del Jordan's drive with Mr. Chamberlain, "maddeningly erotic" before his valedictory performance, "postcoital" afterwards. But this is always recognized as a particular relationship, a particular result of circumstances and emotions. Because of this, because the solid reality underpins every response to it, several layers of reality can exist at once, as Del realizes during this same drive: "My mother inhabited a different layer of reality from the one I had got into now."

It is in fact this solid centre which frees Munro to explore so fully the complexity and integrity of the inner worlds of the characters who exist within this particular physical landscape. Much of the movement and creative tension of her work flows from her ability to lay these inner worlds side by side, making each valuable and complete and wonderful in itself:

So lying alongside our world was Uncle Benny's world like a troubling distorted reflection, the same but never at all the same. In that world people could go down in quicksand, be vanquished by ghosts or terrible ordinary cities; luck and wickedness were gigantic and unpredictable; nothing was deserved, anything might happen; defeats were met with crazy satisfaction. It was his triumph, that he couldn't know about, to make us see.

All through *Lives of Girls and Women* the particular integrity of these separate and sometimes fantastic worlds is explored, is celebrated. One does not cancel out the other; their very juxtaposition forces us always to explore the nature of their relationship and of the solid reality at their centre.

In the "Flat Roads" section of *Lives of Girls and Women,* Uncle Benny marries Madeleine, the "mail-order bride" who appears in the eyes of the others to be seriously and dangerously "crazy" as well as—more seriously in the eyes of Del's mother—guilty of child-abuse. Yet Ada Jordan's reaction to the situation is juxtaposed with a seemingly unrelated description of the foxes:

At this time of year the foxes were having their pups. If an airplane from the Air Force Training School on the lake came over too low, if a stranger appeared near the pens, if anything too startling or disruptive occurred, they might decide to kill them. Nobody knew whether they did this out of blind irritation, or out of roused and terrified maternal feeling—could they be wanting to take their pups, who still had not opened their eyes, out of the dangerous situation they might sense they had brought them into, in these pens? They were not like domestic animals. They had lived only a very few generations in captivity.

This is not given, I think, to justify Madeleine, but something is admitted here, acknowledged, as it is much later in the story "The Ottawa Valley" where Aunt Lena is described as a woman who beats her children out of the fear that they will grow up lazy or stupid otherwise. The ambiguous, contradictory nature of maternal feelings is allowed into the open. It is seen as part of the flat, often unsatisfactory reality of women's experience which persists behind all our moral reactions, just as Madeleine persists, as a particular woman in specific circumstances, behind the fantasic stories the other characters created around her.

In Munro's development of character, we are never far from the persistent reality of their physical bodies. Women's bodies changed and marked by childbirth, fat, grimy skin, the smells of hair and breath and sweat are as much a definition of the characters as their thoughts, their beliefs and their interactions. This is particularly powerful in relation to her explorations of how women come to terms with themselves as physical beings, their sexuality and their relations to men. It flows directly, I believe, from the statement quoted earlier about the clarity of vision afforded to women by their position in society. In this case, it related more specifically to their particular biology, which allows women to confront directly both their vulnerability and their ability to remain in touch with many layers of experience (the self as daughter, potential mother). On the other side, men in becoming part of a patriarchal culture, learn to deny their vulnerability; they are forced to deny those weaker, younger selves which were once dominated by the woman as mother. This recognition of the differences between women's ability to maintain their various selves, and men's need to deny or control them, is particularly important in Munro's development of several themes.

As she explores her developing sexuality, Del Jordan is able to hold its many aspects together because, at the same time, she is always aware of her body. She worries about being fat; she loves books "where the heroine's generous proportions were tenderly, erotically described." She thinks of herself romantically, ceremoniously: "I liked looking at the reproduction of Cezanne's 'Bathers' in the art supplement of the encyclopedia, then at myself naked in the glass. But the insides of my thighs quivered; cottage cheese in a transparent sack." And although she enjoys literary descriptions of sex, she comments: "Books always compared it to something else, never told about it by itself." As Mr. Chamberlain had shown her, "people take along a good deal—flesh that is not overcome but has to be thumped into ecstasy, all the stubborn puzzle and dark turns of themselves."

It is this solid understanding, I think, that makes Del's response to her mother's grave speech about the lives of girls and women, her rejection of its assumption that women are somehow damageable and in need of protection, more than adolescent bravado. Or perhaps, her response forces us to recognize that adolescent bravado has a solid base in reality. For she seems to understand not only the limitations, but also the powers of her body and this understanding is the key to her view of the relationship with Garnet French:

Nothing that could be said by us would bring us together; words were our enemies. What we knew about each other was only going to be confused by them. This was the knowledge that is spoken of as "only sex" or "physical attraction." I was surprised, when I thought about it—am surprised still— at the light, even disparaging tone that is taken, as if this was something that could be found easily, every day.

Again, something is acknowledged here, something that many of us, in our attempts to build "enlightened" relationships with men, tend to minimize or even deny. But because Del does not deny it, because she acknowledges its power as well as its limits, she is able to resist when Garnet attempts to move the relationship to another level, as he does in the final baptizing scene:

I felt amazement, not that I was fighting with Garnet but that anybody could have made such a mistake, to think he had real power over me. I was too amazed to be angry, I forgot to be frightened, it seemed to me impossible that he should not understand that all the powers I granted him

57

were in play, that he himself was – in play, that I meant to keep him sewed up in his golden lover's skin forever, even if five minutes before I had talked about marrying him. This was as clear as day to me, and I opened my mouth to say whatever would make it clear to him, and I saw that he knew it all already....

Garnet has seen the true nature of their relationship and its limitations, but his initial reaction has been to deny it, to move beyond it by controlling Del either through marriage, or, as she realizes in the water, by possibly drowning her. In doing so, he denies as well that self which existed within the relationship as a golden, playful lover. Del does neither. She allows the relationship as part of her experience and her place in it as part of herself. Her realization that it is over is not a denial of its importance nor of Garnet's.

Men and women inhabit different worlds; they grant and withold power; they struggle and cause each other pain. In exploring male-female relationships, Munro does not deny that women suffer, that women are vulnerable, but her women have as well a sense of strength and power that has to do directly with the fact that they do not deny any part of their experience or reject any part of themselves.

This is explored in a more complex way in the short story "Boys and Girls." As the child in the story approaches adolescence she realizes: "The word *girl* had formerly seemed to me innocent and unburdened, like the word *child*; now it appeared that it was no such thing. A girl was not, as I had supposed, simply what I was; it was what I had to become." Munro recognizes, certainly, the vulnerability, the oppressiveness of being a girl. There is also in the story a subtle and complex sense of it as an affirmation. When the child frees the horse she realizes: "I was on Flora's side, and that made me no use to anybody, not even to her. Just the same, I did not regret it; when she came running at me and I held the gate open, that was the only thing I could do."

58

An acceptance of limits, a coming to terms with them, is not necessarily a weakness. It is her father who dismisses *her* with the words "She's only a girl" and her brother, proud of his first kill, who forgets that he was once afraid of the dark.

Men lack the ability to acknowledge these weaker, younger selves. In some of the stories in *Something I've Been Meaning to Tell You* Munro explores that lack. In these stories, men are often seen as mysterious, half-formed, essentially inexplicable. They are seen, in fact, as women are often seen in stories written by men. But it is not simply a matter of turning tables, reversing roles. The women who perceive and describe these men have a particular sense of themselves as altogether different from their male counterparts and this affects what they see in men and, more important, how they handle what they see.

An excellent example of this is the story entitled "Material." On one level "Material" explores how a male writer arranges aspects of reality in fiction and how a woman who is not a writer sees and arranges the same material in her own life. But on another level it is objectively a story written by a woman and therefore a concrete example of how she arranges reality in fiction.

An earlier short story entitled "The Office" deals with this theme in a somewhat simpler, certainly more ironic, way. The woman writer is eventually driven from her office by her over-curious landlord and his bizarre accusations. It ends by making the two types of creativity almost parallel:

Mr. Malley with his rags and brushes and a pail of soapy water, scubbing in his clumsy way, his deliberately clumsy way, at the toilet walls, stooping with difficulty, breathing sorrowfully, arranging in his mind the bizarre but somehow never quite satisfactory narrative of yet another betrayal of trust. While I arrange words, and think it is my right to be rid of him.

59

In "Material," the parallelism is replaced by something else, a subtler, more dynamic tension between the woman narrator and the ex-husband who is a writer. The tension is created through her reaction, not only to the story he writes, but also to her memories of its objective basis in a reality they shared.

The story begins with a somewhat tongue-in-cheek description of the wives of writers: "Their lives are concerned with food and mess and houses and cars and money. They have to remember to get the snow tires on and go to the bank and take back the beer bottles, because their husbands are such brilliant, such talented, incapable men, who must be looked after for the sake of the words that will come from them." This is followed by a description of the women who do admire writers, who are married to engineers and businessmen and take up literature as penance for their husbands' philistinism. The narrator is herself married to an engineer.

The core of the story, however, is her memories of Dotty, and the events surrounding Dotty, which are also the events surrounding the disintegration of her first marriage. Her memories are clear and precise; she remembers too how she served the details up to Hugo as possible material, although he did not use it. We are made aware of how this woman, like the women she described earlier, relates to her writer-husband. She deals with reality; she fixes it for him, protects and feeds his "creativity," just as she protects him from Dotty's noise.

In the end, however, she falls short of her objective. On the issue of the pump and the flooded basement she is unable to play out her wifely role: "... I was not able fully to protect or expose him, only to flog him with blame, desperate sometimes, feeling I would claw his head open to pour my vision into it, my notion of what had to be understood."

The marriage counsellor tells them they are incompatible; it is an incompatibility not only of personalities, but also of roles, of visions, of relations to life.

And this is the crux of her reaction to Hugo's story, written years later, in which Dotty is a central figure. She admires the story, admires its honesty and its technique. She considers writing a letter acknowledging her appreciation of it. But her appreciation of the story is undercut by another, equally strong perception:

> At the same time, at dinner, looking at my husband Gabriel, I decided that he and Hugo are not really so unlike. Both of them have managed something. Both of them have decided what to do about everything they run across in this world, what attitude to take, how to ignore or use things. In their limited and precarious ways they both have authority. The are not *at the mercy*. Or think they are not. I can't blame them, for making whatever arrangements they can make.

The letter she begins to write comes from this vision: *"This is not enough, Hugo. You think it is, but it isn't. You are mistaken, Hugo. That is not an argument to send through the mail. I do blame them. I envy and despise."*

What she despises, I think, is the way in which she sees men controlling reality by cutting out what they cannot use, denying it even in themselves. What she is beginning to see — and what the structure of the story, on another level, exemplifies — is that women do not do this. They are able to hold everything in a kind of tension in which varying, often contradictory elements, "scraps and oddments, useless baggage even" exist and have their own integrity. It is a painful juxtaposition, but a way of coming to terms.

In Munro's eyes, men do not come to terms with what they cannot control and understand in this way, even in their relationships with women. They relate as Ewart, the self-controlled father of the dead boy in "Memorial" relates to Eileen, his wife's sister, when he sleeps with her: "He lies in her to acknowledge, to yield — but temporarily, safely — to whatever has got his son, whatever cannot be spoken of in his house ... a woman's body. Before and during the act they seem to invest this body with certain individual powers.... Afterwards it appears that they have changed their minds, they wish it understood that such bodies are interchangeable."

How women relate to men is explored in another way in "Tell Me Yes or No." Again, the story works on many levels, its complexity intensified by the fact that the major events in it are explicitly presented as an invention of the woman writer.

She imagines the death of a lover, a man who is important, not only in himself but also because he links her with her younger, innocent self. It is partly through him, and through her relationship with him, that she holds these selves together: "If I could kindle love then and take it now there was less waste than I had thought. Much less than I had thought. My life did not altogether fall away in separate pieces, lost."

In the fantasy surrounding the man's death and her reaction to it, another woman emerges, who is also in love with him although she does not know he is dead. She thinks she has been deserted: "She suffers according to rules we all know, which are meaningless and absolute. When I think of her I see all this sort of love as you must have seen, or see it, as something going on at a distance; a strange, not even pitiable, expenditure; unintelligible ceremony in an unknown faith. Am I right, am I getting close to you, is that true?"

The ceremonies of suffering which this woman performs are similar to those which the narrator imagines herself performing in reaction to her lover's death. The love, the "unknown faith" which she sees at a distance, as men see it, is in fact her own suffering, her own love. She is aware of herself both as subject and as object in the relationship.

But she also remembers that it was the man who first talked of love; "*you were the one who said it first.*" If the ceremonies of women are unintelligible to men, how are women to understand men who first make a claim of love and then deny its effects? "How are we to understand you?" she asks, the "we" uniting her with the imaginary jilted woman, with that distanced but equally real part of herself, just as earlier, she identified with the case histories in women's magazines.

Never mind. I invented her. I invented you, as far as my purposes go. I invented loving you and I invented your death. I have my tricks and my trap doors, too. I don't understand their workings at the present moment, but I have to be careful, I won't speak against them.

In acknowledging that this is all invention, she allows as well the self who would invent such a man, acknowledges the need to come to terms with this aspect of experience. She does not deny this need; she is aware that the process by which women order their lives is different from that of men; she does not completely understand it, but she is aware of its power.

The juxtapositioning of different types of women, of parts and counterparts is a constant theme in Munro's work. The movement is always toward holding all of them in tension, celebrating their separate realities. In *Lives of Girls and Women*, Del and Naomi move out into their separate lives with affection and respect for each other. The awkward young girl in "Red Dress – 1946" recognizes another part of herself in Mary Fortune just as she recognizes that for the time she herself is as "boy crazy" as the girls Mary Fortune despises. Often the juxtapositioning involves a recognition of treachery, of bad faith, as it does in the relationship between the little girl in "Day of the Butterfly" and her dying friend Myra or between Eileen and June in "Memorial," but even this recognition is not denied. What cannot be fully faced is held still, examined, kept, even as its limits are recognized. Munro's ability to do this with different characters is centred I think in her recognition that within each woman many contradictory selves exist simultaneously.

"My mother had not let anything go. Inside that self we knew, which might at times appear blurred a bit, or side-tracked, she kept her younger selves strenuous and hopeful...."

Del is not always pleased with the many selves her mother maintains – the unromantic housewife, the odd woman with her outlandish opinions – but part of her development through the novel is a coming to terms with her own contradictory selves and with the fact that her mother is part of her identity as well.

For at the centre of our attempt to maintain our many selves within us, is an understanding that within each of us always, lies the twin identity of daughter and mother. Munro explores this relationship, painfully, in two stories about mothers and daughters, "The Peace of Utrecht" and "The Ottawa Valley." In the former, the daughter, now herself a mother, returns to her mother's home, to herself as daughter once more, and begins to come to terms with the guilt surrounding her mother's death. Here, her awareness of the potential strength of her dead mother's continued domination is embodied in her two aunts, and their attitude toward her. And her own tenuous attempts to come to terms with her guilt, to free herself from her mother, is intensified by her sister Maddy's inability to do so.

"The Ottawa Valley" works in another way. Here, the narrator remembers a childhood trip with her mother to the place of her mother's childhood, during which she is confronted with her mother as a child. Through Aunt Dody, improbable stories of her mother's youth are presented. She is forced to explore the bare physical reality of her mother's old home, just as, in Aunt Dody's account of her own jilting she must confront the contradiction between this matter-of-fact version and her mother's more romantic rendition of it.

Toward the end of the story she must also confront yet another aspect of her own mother-daughter identity. Her mother, already in the first stages of Parkinson's disease, moves toward the possibility of a "second childhood" in which the daughter will be forced to play mother, a fear intensified for her by Aunt Dody's grim account of taking care of *her* mother.

By juxtaposing these events and memories, the inter-

64

relationship between mother and daughter, Munro explores concretely the juxtaposition of selves (daughter, potential mother, mother of a daughter) that exists always and powerfully in every woman. She recognizes as well that it is impossible for women to cancel any of these identities without at the same time denying a part of themselves.

In the incident outside the church, where the mother sacrifices her own appearance and offers her daughter the needed safety pin, the daughter remains too sure of her own rights as a child to thank her. But the mature woman, remembering this incident, sees now how her mother must have planned her outfit, planned her appearance, just as she herself now does. She stands now as mother to her own self as daughter. She cannot deny either.

And again, when the daughter pesters her mother about her illness, she is demanding the impossible, a release from her dual role, for as a child, she believes this is something one consents to, or denies:

I demanded of her now that she turn and promise me what I needed.

But she did not do it. For the first time she held out altogether against me. She went on as if she had not heard, her familiar bulk ahead of me turning strange, indifferent. She withdrew, she darkened in front of me, although all she did in fact was keep on walking along the path that she and Aunt Dodie had made when they were girls running back and forth to see each other; it was still there.

At the end of the story, Munro interjects directly to explore the powerful nature of this relationship even further:

The problem, the only problem, is my mother. And she is the one of course that I am trying to get; it is to reach her that this whole journey has been undertaken. With what

65

purpose? To make her off, to describe, to illumine, to cele-
brate, to *get rid* of her; and it did not work, for she looms too
close, just as she always did. She is heavy as always, she
weighs everything down, and yet she is indistinct, her
edges melt and flow. Which means she has stuck to me as
close as ever and refused to fall away, and I could go on, and
on, applying what skills I have, using what tricks I know,
and it would always be the same.

Whether I read this paragraph as a statement about the
limitations of writing as therapy or an acknowledgement of the
impossibility of getting beyond not only our biological
mothers but also the duality of our identity as women, I used
to see it always as a statement of failure. Defeat.

In "The Peace of Utrecht" the narrator describes her
daughter's reaction to seeing her childhood home: "And I felt
that my daughter's voice expressed a complex disappointment
– to which, characteristically, she seemed resigned, or even
resigned *in advance*; it contained the whole flatness and
strangeness of the moment in which is revealed the source of
legends, the unsatisfactory, apologetic and persistent reality."

There is something of that complex disappointment in
Munro's own statement about her mother. But as I read it now,
in the context of the rest of her fiction, I see that it contains
something more. It acknowledges the simple, flat reality of
women's lives, acknowledges the power, the primacy of the
mother that exists within each of us. In allowing the mother,
we allow the existence of our other selves as well. We have not
been forced, as men often have, to deny, to control, to fear
these selves we do not yet understand or may not yet like.
Many of us have felt for a long time that this was a weakness.
We are only now beginning to see it as a strength.

The strength of Munro's fiction is centred in this persistent
reality. She gives us mothers and daughters, old women, awkward adolescents, jilted mistresses, gives them to us in all the
strangeness and commonness of their particular situations. She

acknowledges them, allows them even, in a way that gives us the chance to acknowledge them – these many women we are and could possibly be – in ourselves.

Ten Years of Literature:
A Writer at the Canada Council

Naim Kattan

In 1967, when I agreed to join the staff of the Canada Council, I stipulated that I must retain my freedom to write. From then on it was up to me to define the boundary-line between my official duties and my self-expression. The experiment seems to me–tentatively, of course–to have been successful as far as I am concerned. To combine the management of a literary program with the pursuit of an individual literary career raises manifold questions, with an interest beyond the particular case. The relationship between one's personal taste and one's responsibilities to a community, the impact of public funds on the artist's freedom of expression – in more general terms, the relation between culture and the state – these are some of the problems I live with every day. To speak more precisely, the position I occupy has put me in daily contact with literary life in both languages and in the various regions of the country. I deal with writers and with the whole commercial and industrial structure surrounding their work–publishing-houses and periodicals. I don't find that this gets in the way of my own writing. I have noticed that frustrated artists make the worst arts administrators; watching project after project undertaken and completed, they wince at thoughts of their own unfinished work; ultimately they are haunted by the work that will never come off. For such artists the works of others become a constant reminder that they are out of the race, that they have left the group, that at best they are powerless spectators. Their strong temptation, then, is to translate service, which is their job, into power. The artist may then become submerged in the administrator; and the administrator, like a parent who seeks fulfilment through his child, and with all the unwholesome expectations that that entails, seeks indirectly and often unconsciously to impose his own artistic dreams on others. And since the work dreamed about is never the work achieved, the expectations are perverted in advance, the demands ill-founded.

Because I myself have work in progress, I understand from the inside the vulnerability of ambition, the uncertainty of any achievement, and the hard labour required. My position has one inconvenience: I have to do without all the perquisites available to other writers—grants, prizes, translation subsidies, and so on. But that is not the main point. My job enables me to gauge all that the Council, and through the Council the state, does for the artist. In spite of all that may be said for the democratic system as a protector of freedom of speech, the fact remains that a state that is increasingly the source of funds and perquisites is no less a menace. Liberties can be eroded subtly, quite without conscious will or a concerted plan. The fact that governments determine needs and set priorities gives them scope to choose those artists who best answer those needs. It's easy to slip into such practices, and we know what they can lead to: the totalitarian countries give us grievous examples every day. The regulators of conscience take good care of those who subscribe to their slogans; as for the rest, they neglect them, starve them and ultimately force them into silence. A democratic state cannot go as far as that, but its ability to give help, its right to interfere, expose it to numerous temptations to impose directives on thought and on artistic expression.

The means of doing this can be especially insidious in the

hands of unconscious idealogues and artists *manqués*. Creative artists who claim to have the answers, who declare precisely defined aims, are often mistaken, but that doesn't matter if the result is a body of work. Such a body of work contains its own answers, and society is free to derive instruction or pleasure from them according to its needs. As long as those needs don't become a pretext for laying down a way for the artist to follow, the dynamic of a relationship between art and society will be maintained.

My experience leads me to two conclusions. First, governments feel comfortable when artistic institutions that depend on public funds are headed by what are customarily called "administrators," whose neutrality is a warrant of efficiency and right-mindedness. Now, without an understanding of the artistic process one cannot pursue genuine cultural objectives. And anyway, the cultural objectives are laid down by politicians. In the short term, the control that this puts in the hands of governments relieves them of many anxieties and lulls them into the comfortable illusion that power is theirs alone, and that their proclamation of a cultural mission gives meaning and purpose to their authority. This is the easy way. In the long term, the dynamic voices are reduced to silence and cultural life itself sinks into paralysis. It is incumbent on the artists, then, to assert their presence, to participate in the decisions that affect them. One of the great advantages of democracy is precisely this, that it makes such participation possible; it is the laziness, or the default, of artists that gives free rein to the appetites of the regulators of conscience.

My second conclusion concerns the direct ascendancy of the politicians over culture. I have learned to beware of it. With the best intentions, politicians find it almost irresistible to impose taste, opinion and ideology once they become the artistic and cultural decision-makers. That is why it is necessary to multiply the institutions, the intermediary cultural bodies responsible for distributing state aid without depending directly on government. A minister must not have the power to deprive an artist of state aid for reasons defined by him alone, even though they may be artistic reasons. It is for the cultural community itself to assess its members' merits. The errors and injustices that that community is liable to commit are inherent in all human relations, when individuals are called upon to judge the merits of other individuals. Every work of art runs the risk of being misunderstood – or overvalued. But that is a human phenomenon, and by extension an artistic phenomenon. Moral, religious or political interference, imposed from outside by an authority that doesn't belong to the artistic community, is another matter altogether. At first sight, the system we have seems untidy, teeming with contradictions and uncertainty. In fact, that is its strength; it is fitted to the dynamic of artistic creation. The Canada Council, a creature of the state, is neither a screen between government and the artistic élite nor the state's weapon for exerting its power over the cultural world. It is a link in the socio-cultural chain, between the needs of culture and the needs of the state; its ultimate beneficiary is society as a whole. The existence of provincial councils and other bodies does not add to the confusion, even though it may involve some duplication of functions. A multiplicity of decision-making centres is a safeguard for freedom.

I was appointed to the Council to start a separate department for literature. Until then the arts had been treated as one entity, and it had become a question of volume; it was clear that one person could no longer deal with music, painting, theatre and literature. But the diversification of responsibilities was not merely a matter of dividing up a given quantity of work, for there was a qualitative as well as a quantitative change. Publishers in English Canada were in large part distributors of foreign books, and were often branches of British houses. In French Canada they were offshoots of the Church, concerned mainly with scholarly works. There were also a few free spirits, still at the cottage-industry stage, who pushed their audacity so far as to publish other newcomers, authors who didn't preach intellectual safety or moral conformity.

My arrival at the Council coincided with two important phenomena. French-Canadian literature was being transformed into Quebec literature. And in English Canada small publishing-houses, mostly founded by writers, were taking over from established firms whose basic assumption was that they could not risk publishing too many books – fiction and poetry especially – that would show a loss. This foreshadowed a new awareness that was to lead to the takeover of a culture by its authors and craftsmen. With a few years' time-lag, English-Canadian literature followed in the footsteps of Quebec literature.

In Quebec, nobody apologized any more for reading the poets, novelists and essayists of the country. It even became trendy to read only native writers; but the passion – and the need – were real.

The poets showed the way. Voices heard by few during the fifties were amplified in the sixties. And in Quebec, bards became standard-bearers. For these voices to reach their public, some stimulus had to be given to publishing. For a few years a service intended to give a helping hand to writers had to engage in assistance to commercial publishing enterprises. Commercial? The word shouldn't be stressed; most of these craftsmen were operating at a loss.

In English Canada too, the young publishers were daring freebooters. Their strength lay in their consciousness of an awakening. They were the heroes of new departures. It was not yet a matter of nationalism, it was a matter of generation. A new stage had been reached. In the thirties, and still more in the forties, English Canada had produced, ahead of French Canada, a whole galaxy of poets and other writers of the left who sang of future births and denounced the abominations of a society of poverty and insecurity. But the new wave didn't imitate the ideologues and social reformers. What it discovered was neither a political reality nor a new vocabulary; it was a whole new language. Writers no longer took their lead from

London; could no longer be grouped, as Commonwealth writers, in one family of heart and mind.

America confronted them, in all its diversity and power. It beckoned to creative people, flaunting all the seductions of fame. But the price was clearly too high: it implied the disappearance of all dissenting voices. A continent on the march was not tolerant of autonomies, still less of differences. At most, it gave free rein to regionalisms, as being necessary components of the whole. In other words, the young English-Canadian poets were compelled to proclaim their separate identity—even though their style was not merely close to, but similar to, almost identical with, their southern neighbour's. This made itself felt first in the West, in Vancouver—understandably, since it was there that not only spatial proximity but a shared attitude to space opened the door to all kinds of simplistic and facile combinations and confusions.

What happened was actually the transformation of an area into a locality, the rediscovery of Canada as something other than an extension of Europe—a legally constituted dominion, but really an entity so abstract that its inhabitants had not made it into a habitat.

Regionalism? Yes, in the most precise but also the most positive sense of the word. For the poets, for writers generally, Canada is a set of habitats, each with its own characteristics, its own peculiarities, chosen and developed by its people. The poets were the first to speak for themselves and identify themselves with specific regions, even if they were able to incorporate other regions into their consciousness and express them too. Alden Nowlan is a New Brunswick poet, just as Purdy and Souster are Ontario poets, and the publishers of *Tish* wanted to identify themselves as a West Coast group. To differentiate themselves from the United States, writers had to discover themselves in their own milieus and to reveal their regions to themselves and to others. It was recognized that the Americans could attain the dimension of time—that is, history—only by exploring space and setting bounds to it. They were

Southerners, Midwesterners or Easterners. And their regions were not solely geographical ones; one can be a Jewish, Italian or Catholic novelist, forming human regions based on membership in religious or ethnic groups. Canadians too identified themselves as Jews or Ukrainians quite as readily as Easterners or Westerners. In Quebec, Catholicism freed itself from the abstract manifestations that it had superimposed on social and ethnic realities, to rediscover its original nature: the spiritual relation between man and man, between man and the real world.

The writers' rediscovery of Canada revealed a hitherto unknown Canada. The West ceased to be simply the new prairie, the new cities, the soil to be turned, the gold to be sought. It was a human realm, where people toiled, and people were bored, and behind a courteous exterior there were rumblings of thwarted violence. In Acadia, the social statements of Antonine Maillet were marked by historical memory and a cheerfully mocking wit.

In Quebec, young novelists such as Roch Carrier and Victor-Lévy Beaulieu were not content to restate the supremacy of the group, born of minority solidarity and the instinct for self-defence. Quebec itself was made up of regions.

The face of Canada defies simple description. Its territory is vast and the human communities that people it are far from uniform. The poets and novelists revealed a country of manifold resources and unsuspected human complexities. We had got into the habit of seeing it from the outside, like visitors from abroad. Now we were looking at it from the inside and we recognized that we could grasp only parts of it, that our vision was fragmentary and there was no obvious overall pattern. A rich country, but a fragile one.

During the sixties, novelists and poets in Quebec were calling for political independence. We at the Canada Council lived with the drama of their rejection of the historical Canada and its federal system. Because it administers the Governor General's Awards, the Council was in the thick of the fray. Our position was that an artist had complete freedom of expression and that our criterion was merit, with no ideological or political implications; it was possible to be a Quebec separatist and a first-rate Canadian writer at the same time. Some writers, by refusing the award, repudiated this attitude. But we refused to fall into the trap. It would have been easy to change the rules of the game, and choose less recalcitrant prizewinners, more pliable juries; which in the long run would have destroyed the freedom, not only of the separatists but of all the others. Once you establish any criterion other than the artistic ones for rewarding merit you open the door to every sort of high-handedness. We had to stand firm so that the whole structure would not collapse. And it stood, in spite of storms. It was clear to me that in their refusal and by their demand for independence the French-Canadian writers were asserting their attachment to the country, their love of a land whose boundaries they defined. There were no more dreams of a distant France or of a wealthy America; amidst the tumult and the shouting, they were declaring for this country. "This country," of course, didn't mean the whole of Canada; and this too exposed its fragility.

And then Margaret Atwood published *Survival*. This was the rallying-cry. The literature, and through it the historical and political reality, of Canada were revealed, perhaps not as a totality, but at least as a collectivity, though a fragile one. Canada was not merely a constitutional dream, a legal construction; it was a human reality based on human choices and historical decisions. Atwood agreed with neither the choices nor the decisions, but beneath her apparent destructiveness even Atwood was saying, in the midst of the controversy, that the country did exist by the will of those who painfully built it, that its regions were not geographical, or rather not merely geographical. Its parts made up a whole, and it was from this whole that each region derived its full significance. These parts did not negate each other; they complemented each other, even if the overall pattern had, in Atwood's eyes, a negative

75

character. The book's success is more important, more significant than its author's particular arguments. Canadians, young Canadians largely, were reading the authors of all regions, and recognizing themselves in them. Here is the real country. It is not a matter of celebrating its beauty; it is an affirmation of belonging, a self-commitment. The country's future will depend on whose who recognize it and recognize themselves in it. Many of these have been dubbed nationalists, because they were trying to define a territory; their self-affirmation in terms of differences turned into hostility to the United States. This is a marginal phenomenon; none of these writers claim that their country is superior to others. It is different, and it is its own.

I have said that the harbingers were the poets. Over the last ten years I have noticed a trend: whereas in the late sixties poets constituted the majority of applicants for Council funds – anglophone as well as francophone – at the beginning of the seventies novelists came forward in greater numbers. Publishers, falling into step, were opening their doors to young novelists whose idiom was at once new and traditional: traditional because they were discovering their own land, and new because they expressed it in their own style. They were alone in their enterprise, but they enrolled themselves in history and saw themselves as members of a collectivity that eluded quick or easy definition.

The poets announced the country, the novelists described it. And then it was the dramatists' turn. In Quebec, led by Michel Tremblay, they set out to go further than the poets and novelists, or rather in a different direction. Not content with declaring or describing the country, they made it talk, they let the people of the country speak. The speech was direct and authentic, certainly; but it was not an exact reproduction of reality; it was one dimension of it. Later, the English-Canadian dramatists followed a similar, parallel road. They began by perceiving, within a single country, the peculiarities of the regions, and within each region a group solidarity that did not

76

preclude individual voices, even discordant ones. Group life consists of exchanges: ties are strengthened in the course of conflicts and confrontations. This is the social game, the human game – theatre, in a word. The country is alive. The writers declare it, describe it, and listen to it speaking. The voices are fragmented, yet they assure a collective vision, a living reality; for it is seen, and observed freely and honestly, indeed candidly. In the picture of the country as a whole, the writers are scattered, sometimes isolated. The totality is real only so far as its poets remain alive in their individuality but firm in their attachment to the totality.

Translated by I.M. Owen

The Twilight of Self-Consciousness

David McFadden

For the knowledge of the self-apart-from-God is an abyss
down which the soul can slip writhing and twisting in all
the revolutions of the unfinished plunge of self-awareness,
now apart from God, falling fathomless, fathomless, self-
consciousness wriggling writhing deeper and deeper in all
the minutiae of self-knowledge, downwards, exhaustive,
yet never, never coming to the bottom, for there is no
bottom...
> —D.H. Lawrence, "Only Man," *Last Poems* (1929).

The highways are actually arteries carrying the lifeblood to
unarticulated primeval form using cities, oil refineries, jet
and auto engines, factories, and any form of fossil fuel con-
sumption to slowly replace the present composition of the
atmosphere with the chemical composition of the atmosphere some 200 million years ago. After a certain critical
point this atmosphere will become capable of generating
the life-forms essential to this ancient form
> —Christopher Dewdney, "Sol du Soleil,"
> *A Palaeozic Geology of London, Ontario* (1973)

Occasionally, even, the poem is nothing more than a day-dream the writer has lulled you into while he is in an adjacent room torturing himself with magnets. The presence of the picnic, taking place somewhere offstage from this poetry, accounts for the strange occurrence of gastronomic items which tend to drift into the plane of our logic and likewise or counter-likewise get digested without the poet's or the reader's knowledge
— Robert Fones, "Memo from 'The Sense of Impending Doom Society,'" *The Forest City* (1974).

When D. H. Lawrence said that "if men were as much men as lizards are lizards they'd be worth looking at" he wasn't talking about wattles or bright colours. He was talking about the same thing he was talking about when he said: "All that matters is to be at one with the living God." He was talking about what Robert Fones calls an "adjacent room," a way of being that preceded ordinary self-consciousness and that will come back to us when we've had enough of self-consciousness, when we finally decide we've been plunging into Lawrence's bottomless pit long enough.

If a man could be as much man, or for that matter if a woman could be as much woman, as a lizard is a lizard, what would that mean? What would he or she be like? The whole panoply of Lawrence's and Christ's moral precepts comes into play here and that's far from enough. The programming, the conditioning of the last three millennia would vanish like a dream and we would come into constant possession of all the beauties of the religious, the poetic, life. And even that's not enough.

Lawrence would have found Christopher Dewdney and Robert Fones "worth looking at" for they are two men who are quietly living that kind of life to the full—and writing about it. The writers we care about today are those using language to delineate a universe that has been created by the force of their

79

own individual human characters. To do this well requires the sort of awesome humility and naturalness of spirit which Lawrence seems to be talking about in his poem about the lizards and which he seems to have developed only in the last few months of his life. Dewdney and Fones seem to have been *born* with these qualities. And even though they're still in their twenties – and in a sense belong to the twenty-first century – they've already produced a body of work that mocks the Canadian painter Harold Town's famous statement about the modernist ego: "If you don't think you're the greatest you might as well quit."

It was August and Dewdney was sunning in my backyard, like a lizard. For some reason I went up to him and handed him an Irving Layton poem. I don't think he'd ever seen one before. It struck me as being a fairly average Irving Layton poem, not particularly good, not particularly bad. "Gaaawd," said Dewdney when he'd stared at it for a while in the bright sun, drawing out the "o" with a hint of annoyance. "The only thing this is good for is prime-time TV." He adjusted his tan bikini briefs and lay back down in the sun.

Later I happened to ask Dewdney and Fones why they never publish in literary magazines. "I think we respect a humble person more than an ostentatious person," said Dewdney. "It's just a boorish thing to do, to send poems to a magazine."

But there are so many different kinds of humility. Robert Fones was on a bird-watching trip in the vicinity of Collingwood, Ontario, during the Great Canadian Poetry Weekend which was being held at Collingwood. Not only had Fones not been invited, he hadn't even heard of it until he happened to catch something about it on his van radio. He heard a recent Governor General's Award-winning poet being interviewed and he could hear all the partying in the background. "R – sounded so arrogant I couldn't believe it," said Fones. "The whole thing sounded just dreadful. I was glad I wasn't there. But then again deep down I guess I was a little hurt that they hadn't asked me."

Underlying this article is a belief that these two Canadians are part of a Holy Society of post-modern poets who are at the end of the rope existentially, as far as the current range of human existence is concerned. This is not to say they are part of any school, or that the members of this Holy Society all sound alike. I think if there were anyone in the world doing anything similar to what Dewdney or Fones are doing I'd somehow know about it. Rather they're bound by a certain spirituality of direction, a sense they are working each in his own way with something massive, that they are struggling bravely with what will later be perceived as the difficult beginnings of a great change in world consciousness. This change will be widely heralded by AD 2000 but will not be complete until another millennium has passed.

The Holy Society, and I hope I'm not courting their displeasure by saying so, is the first of a wave of mutants that are going to take over the world and take it back to Eden. The takeover will not be political or even cultural. It'll just be something in the air. Lawrence would have been sanctified but the Society doesn't believe in saints. Irving Layton and other artists of the endlessly posturing ego would be just as likely to be sanctified. After all, who can fail to admire those brave old pugilists who keep coming back for more and more like George Chuvalo? It's awesome. It's like having an asthma attack. But it has nothing to do with this happy band of alchemists.

Dewdney and Fones both publish with Coach House Press and the Canadian poet Al Purdy might have had them in mind when he spoke recently of the "gods of sameness at Coach House Press." He should know that only when you stop searching for individuality and originality do you find it. We're into a transcendent sort of individuality here, as we shall see, an individuality so profound one can be forgiven for not immediately noticing it. As far as artistic maturity is concerned I think Dewdney and Fones are on a psychic journey way past the point where one can expect them ever to quit writing, having visions

81

and so on, way past the dangerous point where one either sails or drowns. Earlier on there was a third—John Koegler—but he committed suicide, his neck "slit with great shark gills" as Dewdney says in "I Am the Lord and These Are My Flies."

My dreams confirm what I am saying. During a break I dozed off and dreamt that Dewdney and Fones were on a field trip collecting brightly illuminated objects and bringing them to me. They kept saying, "Here, this is just a small sample of what the new consciousness will be like." They were holding small UFOs that seemed to be totally composed of divine light and small sticks that seemed like fragments of laser beams. There was of course strange music in the air. (Dewdney says that because of relentless psychic drift, the music of Debussy is now directly over Southwestern Ontario.)

Yet I can't afford time here to try to prove how Dewdney and Fones fit into this mythological mutantship, nor am I going to betray the Society by naming names and all that. That would be terribly profane. I'm not a PR man for a new religious organization, and what I say here isn't going to make any difference at all except to my own satisfaction. All I can do is discuss the style and substance of Dewdney and Fones, and indulge in a little gossip about them, in the hope that this will help illuminate their allegedly difficult writings for you should you feel inspired to check them out. I think, however, their reputation for difficulty is simply unfounded. They are basically fun poets, humorous, a pleasure to read with or without understanding. In fact it might be better if you don't understand them. Yet a prominent Vancouver poet, paradoxically one of the most prominent Canadian members of the Holy Society, claims he neither understands nor enjoys Dewdney's poetry. Another prominent Canadian poet, editor and academic refused to host a reading for Christopher Dewdney at the university where he teaches on the grounds that he simply can't understand a word he says. Yet Dewdney's prophecies are easier to grasp then Blake's. Would he have refused a reading for Blake? The League of Canadian Poets (not

82

to be confused with the Holy Society) tried valiantly to set up a 30-reading national tour for Dewdney. They managed to get him *one* reading. Fones, as we shall see, is becoming more accessible to a wider range of readers. But he goes into gales of laughter whenever anyone mentions the League of Canadian Poets.

We discussed their reputation for difficulty. "I certainly like poetry I don't understand," said Fones. "It means you can return to it again and again and walk away with something new each time. That's the beauty of it. So naturally I'm going to want to write it too."

Added Dewdney: "I think it's possible for a writer to write beyond himself. That's the kind of writing we want. And that's clearly distinguishable from someone using ambiguity as a device."

Of course it's clearly distinguishable but how? "That's the automatic editor," says Dewdney. "Bob and I agree *implicitly* on poems that you could give us. You could give us both six books that neither has seen before. And we'd come to the same decision on each book."

Ah, their enviable closeness. There's something fascinating about the notion of two strong writers growing out of the same time and place – time-mates would be the corresponding astrological term – feeding off each other and evolving out of each other for a few youthful years and then emerging unscathed, with neither one dominant.

Robert Fones was born in the east end of London, Ontario, on 10 March, 1949. Christopher Dewdney was born in the west end of the same sedate little city on 9 May, 1951. Fones has now settled in Toronto while Dewdney, after ill-fated attempts to settle in Toronto, Hamilton and Jamaica, is living in London again. As mentioned before, both publish with Toronto's Coach House Press, the navel of Canadian publishing.

Fones has published *Kollages* (1970), mostly visuals, *Anthropomorphiks* (1971) and *The Forest City* (1974). Dewdney has published *Golder's Green* (1970), *A Palaeozoic Geology of London, Ontario* (1973), *Fovea Centralis* (1975), and *Spring Trances* (1978). None of this writing could be called influential yet. But that it will be is as obvious as the changing of the seasons. For there is considerable enthusiasm for their work developing among Anglophone writers in at least three countries. An example of current inner-circle enthusiasm, here's what novelist David Young (*Agent Provocateur*) had to say recently about Dewdney's *Geology* (in conversation): "It was by far the best book of 1973. It should have won every prize going." Of course Young is on the Coach House editorial board. But still.... It's as if we all know their work is great but we don't really know what to say about it. But someone will have to say something eventually and then someone else will say something else and eventually we'll have it all absorbed. One suspects that if Dewdney and Fones were ever included in the normal run of young-Canadian-poet anthologies they would simply make everyone else look so retarded, so hackneyed, so unenlightened that it would be culturally unproductive.

Fones is currently working on a long series of short stories called *Swan-Song*. These involve a character named Bobo who is always a little more naïve, a little more earnest, a little more trusting and a little less bright than the author is himself. Bobo goes to Florida with a camera and an album of old photos taken of him by his parents during a trip they took to Florida when he was a kid. He finds all the same background spots and has himself rephotographed full grown in each. In his van Bobo has installed a Video Scanner (with money he won playing Crown and Anchor at the Canadian National Exhibition) through which he can tell how many turkey vultures or cedar waxwings there are in an x-mile radius of his locale, or what was happening in the immediate area in say 1949 or 1849 or even 2300 BC. And so on. The writing is opening up and becoming more accessible. The individual human being is telling us what he saw during his period of seeming incomprehensibility when he was whisked away by flying saucers. Everything is intact. But it has slowed down and is being recollected in tranquility.

The opposite seems to be holding true in Dewdney's latest work. It is somehow *less* human rather than more, and more into the realm of pure intelligence, into the realm of a spirit so pure and pervasive it's as if a computer were programmed with the music of Debussy and a dictionary and were being asked to use that material to compose poetry. This is *Spring Trances in the Emerald Control Night* which is the first book of Dewdney's projected life-long opus, *A Natural History of Southwestern Ontario*.

Dewdney is also writing something he calls an "espionage science-fiction occult thriller," a long novel he doesn't expect to have finished before 1984. In it young boys have to battle hungry sharks in shallow swimming-pools in order to achieve initiation, and spy rings have mastered the art of astral projection. Dewdney is holding this one pretty close to his vest although he appears to have huge sections completed.

This divergence into totally opposite directions is quite an unexpected phenomenon although we have nothing to gauge it by. Fones and Dewdney have known each other since adolescence and went through a long period in the late nineteen-sixties and early nineteen-seventies when, as Fones says, "It was just very urgent, almost compelling, that we be together as much as we could be." No, it was nothing sexual.

"It seemed we had a lot of work to do together," says Dewdney. "And that's actually what the whole thing was, it was just a lot of work together which seemed to be based on play."

There is something quite mythological going on: an intense classical relationship followed by a friendly parting and a rapid divergence. It's a Cain-Abel situation and we keep expecting one to weaken and die. The survivor will become both, and the corpse will be eaten. It's too horrible to contemplate. They're not actually fighting each other, certainly not overtly. Yet there's no doubt they each have a careful eye on their own elbow space.

Actually the growing idea of audience may have had something to do with the rapid divergence of their paths. "I think any writer who's thinking about people he's writing for," says Dewdney, "has lost a certain kind of essential innocence. Bob and I both experienced that loss at the same time and this alienated us from each other to a certain extent. This occured when other people began to get involved in reading our things and we started being published. You find you have to think about other people and a whole new influence comes into things. It really becomes a bit bizarre. It was nice that we had that free time – it was really precious – the time we knew each other before we were thrown out of Eden."

Dewdney is talking here about what is the rarest human quality of the century: purity. He speaks of its loss but neither writer has really lost much of it yet. Like all rare things, even a small amount is valuable and you have to have a certain amount even to know that you are not as pure as you used to be. They are ten years younger than I am yet whenever I think of them I feel a sense of inspiration, of being encouraged by invisible spirits, of having a lot of catching up to do. They are not beacons, that would be too strong. I'm too old for that. But they are at least candles in the darkening gloom. And forms of purity to contemplate and idealize. I know that my saying this will not embarrass anyone, but I love them both and I love that third person which is their relationship and which haunts my reading of their work. The kind of relationship I never had (sob!), in fact the kind of relationship that no-one ever had before. What other writers who have known each other from childhood could you lump together in one article? (I decided to do the piece when I discovered quite by accident one day that each was bothered a little because of their feeling that I preferred the work of the other. God, I was so touched! As if I mattered!)

"Ah, but they're friends of yours!" someone said. Yes, but

they're friends of mine only because of my love for their writing which caused me to seek them out. What is writing but an extension of your aura, an impression of your fleeting spirit in the sidewalk of eternity? And there is no passion like the passion of one who falls in love with another through his or her writings. It's a passion that transcends time–almost.

"I don't think you'd ever call us everyday people's poets. It's not an archaeology of the present," said Fones at one point. Or was it Dewdney? I forget. Strange too because people don't usually link them together like this. This is the first time their names have ever been linked in print. They claim everyone treats them as individuals and makes nothing of their extraordinary relationship. And so I began thinking perhaps I was insulting them by lumping them together like this. No, no, they said. We love it!

Everyday people's poets? It's true that Dewdney was born in the kind of home surroundings you would expect of someone worthy of the high name of poet. His father is the novelist Selwyn Dewdney (*Wind without Rain*) who also works as a naturalist, teacher, visual artist, anthropologist, archaeologist and art therapist. Christopher's mother, Irene Dewdney, is all that and more. She's also into political organizing. Tell them she also makes a delicious chocolate cake, says my daughter. Okay. She also makes a delicious chocolate cake.

"They're anti-imperialists, pacifists, patrons of the local arts …" says Dewdney of his family. "I see myself as a kind of haemophiliac to regionalism. I'm an inbred regionalist, second generation. I've been through this whole thing." Regionalism in the serious sense, regionalism that is somehow dictated by the most serious writerly concerns imaginable: how to transmute time into eternity, how to allow eternity to express its pleasure on the products of time, how to express the universal ethos that pervades our consciousness when we are at our truest point in time and space, how to adjust the angle of vision so that what is underneath the nose becomes poetry.

"I used to go to Greg Curnoe's studio when I was ten looking for beatniks. I'd been watching Peter Gunn on television and I decided I was a detective and I was going to go around looking for beatniks and Greg Curnoe was the closest I could get to a beatnik. So I used to hang around his studio looking for evidence all the time. Never did find the evidence."

Other beatniks who dropped in and hung around a lot included the poet James Reaney, the painter Norval Morrisseau and the poet Milton Acorn. "Milton used to come around to my folks' place whenever he was in London and boil milk in the electric tea-kettle to make hot chocolate. And he still doesn't know I'm writing today, I'm sure."

Yet out of such a wide range of possible culprits it turns out that it was Fones who first turned Dewdney on to writing. Fones contrasts his own family as "very average, middle-class—father carpenter, mother housewife."

"I realized that Bob was completely serious and I wasn't," says Dewdney. "He was planning to devote his whole life to it. And suddenly I realized what I was here for."

"Both Chris and I have stuff we wrote at age nine or ten," says Fones. "We have many parallels in our childhoods. Just as he can't understand how I could come out of such a straight middle-class family, his concerns seem peculiar in light of his upbringing."

Each was the other's foremost teacher. "Each child has an adult who is the genetic teacher for him, who is destined for him," says Dewdney. "It's just a matter of finding him. But only one child in a thousand finds his real teacher. Bob and I were just designed to interlock and intermix really effectively."

"It seemed like a kind of evolution," says Fones. "Two things had evolved and they got to the point where they were allowed to be conscious and to come together in order to solve some problem consciously before they went back into those parallel lines of evolution."

At times they seem like encyclopedia salesmen dividing up a neighbourhood. "Our early influences were the same—Spicer, Olson, Eliot, Dorn," says Fones. "But we each have our per-

sonal heroes too. Chris gravitated toward the New York school
– O'Hara, Berrigan, Padgett, Brainard – while I stuck with
Dorn and my first love, the Dadaists and the early Surrealist
writers – Rimbaud, Cocteau, Jarry, Ponge. Our outstanding
common ground of course is London, Ontario. This is where
our mythology sprang from. I still get a strong feeling when I
go back, something about memory co-existing with reality.
An overlay. It can be a rich and stimulating thing or it can be
stifling. I prefer it in small doses now. Chris is still there and
obviously London is a vital matrix for him. But I needed a fresh
start. Maybe I'll move back some day. I feel at home in Southern Ontario now much the same as I used to feel at home in
London."

From their respective home bases, though, their territories
still overlap. Fones spends a lot of time at Point Pelee,
birdwatching, painting, working on the Bobo stories far into
the soft night. Yet Dewdney points out in a letter: "Inciden-
tally I introduced Robert to Point Pelee in June 1974. I still
claim it (even though I'm not doing anything with it right
now) and I stayed on the Point (while it was still a park) for
eight days in 1965. (So much for the ongoing battle.)"

Both writers are involved in the process of taking elements
from their sacred environments, their *lebensraum*, and using
these elements as figureheads for various difficult metaphysical
concepts, a set of tabs for easy reference. What they are doing is
creating, to be cynical about it, a whole new set of clichés for
the twenty-first century, giving the poets of the future something to rebel against. You can always tell whether a poet is
really authentic by trying to imagine the whole world talking
the way he does in a generation or two. If you can do that, the
subject is an authentic poet. Strange that most prominent
Canadian poets talk the way Canadians talked a generation or
two *ago*.

This archetype-to-cliché process is already happening with
Dewdney and Fones. It's getting hard to look at a fossil without thinking of Dewdney's work – if you're at all familiar with

it—or to look at any cone-shaped object—from a tornado to an ant-lion mound—without thinking of Fones'.

"I think it's very similar to the formation of language," says Dewdney. "It's like Bob finding something in the cone and building us a whole series of concepts and precepts surrounding the cone. Or I pick up an object like the fossil and build up a whole mythology around it...."

"The symbols that Chris and I are using are quite unique," says Fones. "I think both of us would feel quite threatened if some other book turned up with a cone or a fossil in it. That would be trespassing. In that sense what we are aoing is quite different from what Yeats and the Symbolists were doing. These images have really become a very personal language."

We are talking about what Dewdney calls "a geomantic mnemonics in the sense of something rising from the land like anthropomorphics, concretions (he has a huge concretion in the middle of his living-room floor as round as a bowling ball but about four times as big) and fossils...." But how to keep track of who owns what, who owns the kiwi bird, who the sawblade, who the coelecanth?

"It's not that strict with us of course," says Fones. "We both use tornadoes."

"I got mad one time," says Dewdney, "and went over to Bob's place and asked him not to use any insects in his writing. But what I think I've learned now is that there's only so much of Southwestern Ontario."

These two poets could only have come out of London, Ontario, a small city which over the past 40 years has contributed so much in terms of visual arts. And both Dewdney and Fones are visual artists as well, having had several one-man shows each both in Toronto and London. And their books are loaded with their own visual material, collages, found images. They also have the happy facility of having come to terms equally with their natural and cultural environments, using environmental elements ranging from the Pillsbury Dough

Boy to the Niagara Escarpment to construct statements of the most solid poetic import.

"I see us almost as experiments in evolution," says Fones, "— the first poets to emerge since the extinction of woolly old mammoths like Archibald Lampman. All the old poets have died off. Chris and I have often joked about Southern Ontario in terms of mythological claims. He'll take Kettle Point and I'll take Point Pelee. His book about Lake Erie will appear before mine does. We both have this very real sense of unexplored territory and we're both staking out metaphors left, right and centre. It's like the British and French colonies in Upper Canada. It was crucial to build a fort in a certain area if you wanted control over the area. Hence the first forts at Niagara, Detroit and Sault Ste. Marie. Chris and I are something like that. It's humorous and at the same time it's deadly serious."

I'm getting close to my allotted space and part of me is screaming that I haven't said anything yet, and that I should rip it up and start over. Probably I don't really understand Fones and Dewdney. For instance when Dewdney talks about Remote Control, which is probably his chief trademark, I don't really know what he's talking about. Or perhaps each time the phrase comes up I have a different idea of what he means. At any rate when Dewdney gives a public reading he always wears a special lapel pin with the phrase REMOTE CONTROL printed on it. It's a liberating symbol for him. And he collects stories from the popular press about anything to do with remote control or people who have suffered momentary loss of control, such as runaway-bus drivers.

"This is a very important part of my work," he says. "I've always been concerned with nocturnal animals and that whole idea of night. Remote Control started out as a purely mechanistic concept, i.e., you control a machine from a distance with a box by radio waves.... Remote Control first surfaced as I was writing *Geology,* and I experienced a series of dreams in which a group of people was trying to wrest a manuscript from me. Remote Control then became a very evil religious secret society. I still hold onto it as being an alien group of inhuman superintelligent people who control other unwitting victims as we all are and which is extant right now. People going out of control is somehow very important to me. It's part of my humour. I mean I really hate civilization for what they've done to the animals and what they've done to nature. I really have a profound hatred of mankind. I think that's one of my dominant themes."

Equally difficult yet equally saved by its humorous aspect is Fones' concept of animation, a principle running through his work, a principle that holds things together and is full of meaning but does not exist outside the work and can't be understood or explained. It's part of Fones' pantheon of little men who serve as representatives of this animating power. One of these is the Michelin Tire man who sits perched on the roof of Bobo's van and appears throughout the pages of *Anthropomorphiks*. Fones' favourite little man is probably Bertie Bassett the Liquorice Allsorts man who appears at the doorway in a Robert Fones painting that was used to illustrate the cover of my recent Coach House Press book, *The Poets's Progress*. I'd long admired the picture and asked Bob to sell it to me but he always refused. In his poem "Confessions of the Liquorice Allsorts Eater," Fones refers to Bertie Bassett as "my little Virgil."

"Yes, he's led me into a lot of interesting areas," says Fones. "In a way he's led me to paradise and back. He's a little guide." We don't seem to be able to progress past this point so Dewdney offers help.

"I think Bob's sense of animation is a very important theme. But it's a difficult theme in terms of putting your finger on it. I don't think Bob's ever clearly defined it. But there's something about Bob's sense of objects/beings. That's as far as I can get. And there's something implicitly humorous about it. Cars, machinery, things that man has lent his hand to – they come out of the matrix but not quite far enough –

Then Fones opens his mouth as if in a trance. Whose voice is this? Bob's? Rimbaud's? Bertie Bassett's? "They are everything you want to know but they can't tell you about it," he says. "There's no common language."

During his trip to Europe in 1970, Fones visited the Liquorice Allsorts plant in Sheffield, the Michelin Tire plant in Paris, and Rimbaud's birthplace at Charleville. "I visited a lot of Rimbaud's old haunts and went to his grave. But it wasn't nearly as close as sitting in my room writing about him and thinking about him having existed. I was disappointed."

Not all the difficult-sounding concepts are really that difficult. Manual Precognition is Dewdney's term for the technique he's using in *A Natural History of Southwestern Ontario.*

"Manual Precognition is a piece of writing that is written back through itself. I write ten pages in pencil then erase the parts I don't like. Then I fill in the blanks so that the writing is anticipating itself in the actual text. The leading edge of the writing is carried back through itself in the blanks, the thread through the eye of the needle, the blanks left by the automatic editor."

Manual Precognition, a technique other writers have probably fallen on independently, hasn't been getting much of a reception in Canada as far as Dewdney is concerned. After doing his first three books with Coach House Press, Dewdney "decided to shop around just to see what the market was like, to see if people respected me for my earlier books or not." They apparently didn't. He sent *Spring Trances in the Emerald Control Night* to dozens of Canadian publishers with totally negative results. One of the most prominent publishers on the Canadian scene told him it was the worst manuscript he'd ever seen. "They told me it was dead, fixed, and they didn't like it at all. Yet I got a lot of positive reactions from writers whose taste I trusted: you, Michael Ondaatje, Daphne Marlatt.... So I decided to take the book out of the country and I'm getting fairly positive responses from publishers in both England and the United States. (Note: *Spring Trances in the Emerald Control Night* was published in March 1978 by Geoffrey Young's The Figures Press in Berkeley.) "So I must be getting somewhere. I'm getting all the right people mad and all the right people seem to like it."

Under the work of both lies the quest for illumination, the process of shedding what Lawrence calls the dead skin of self-consciousness. The process is intimate, not for profane eyes, but there are so many levels of profanity and since poetic composition is, in the right hands, a spiritual discipline, one can be both public and private at the same time.

Dewdney is the more cautious of the two. He denies the quest is there then contradicts himself. "I'm always looking at everything in relationship to the fact that mankind will evolve beyond the point we're at now – inevitably – and we're not at a final state of consciousness. And all the writing we're doing will be just so much decoration somehow. I have that constant state behind me." He adds that illumination and writing can't be combined. "You've got two choices in life. To reach Transcendence or experience High Adventure. That is if you're doing anything at all. And you have to sacrifice Transcendence for writing. It's sort of the Sir Galahad role in the sense that the poet will reveal the Grail to others but he will never reveal it to himself."

That goes along with the notion that the last thing a poet will sacrifice is his insane desire to immortalize all that he loves, including himself – maybe especially himself. So any kind of spiritual quest is there on a secondary level, second choice so to speak. And the quest will never be fulfilled because it is impure, choked with vanity, part of the self-immortalization process.

"Chris and I were both impressed initially with Jack Spicer's 'poetry by dictation,'" says Fones. "It was close to a religious discipline–the subversion of the ego to create a state which was more receptive to, for lack of a better term, Divine Inspiration. We accept that challenge. I think that's what Chris means by High Adventure. Like Percival's experiences on the rocky pinnacle before he achieves his vision of the Holy Grail. The Quest itself is High Adventure."

Fones has gone through the process of giving up writing because he felt he could never achieve through it the Transcendence he is seeking. He joined the Divine Light Mission then left it on good terms and resumed writing. His current work seems to bounce deliriously back and forth between analysis and illumination.

"The writing that I admire most is that which describes a kind of religious experience. I think of Rimbaud's *Illuminations*, Spicer's *The Holy Grail*, the parables of the Gnostics. Perhaps they experienced this Transcendence constantly or perhaps only occasionally. But this is why Chris said we would both agree on the merits of a random selection of books, because we would both look for a similar motivation in the writing. Ultimately it is something I want to achieve but I don't feel that you can control it or direct it. In that sense it really doesn't matter what you do with your life...."

During the preparation of this piece I've been in the position of someone standing on the spot where he *knows* treasure is buried. Yet it is too early to begin to dig. That's what it is to talk about young poets. We have a fairly large body of work here yet there is still so much to come that all we can do at this time is watch and wait. This piece is for a more general audience than the poets under consideration are used to. It will be years and years before their work is available in large editions. Yet I hope the preceding sallies will provide some help for the adventurous reader who wants to know now what will be happening later. When all the documents are in then we can begin our sincere attempt at understanding. For now we can only stand back and watch these mysterious flares on the dark horizon.

In its own grey, pragmatic, left-hemispherical way, Canada

provides a hospitable terrain for poets of all hues. Yet it's amazing how much resistance and reluctance there is to the work of Dewdney and Fones, outside their own circle of fervent admirers. The kind of poetry that wins instant acceptance in this country is usually pretty sober, conventional stuff, stuff that stays pretty close to the ground and always has an obvious point to make. Perhaps it's a fear of something that is obviously not rational in any tangible way, not pragmatic, something totally right-hemispherical like the unheard music of Keats or the angels flying in and out of Blake's sun. "Take it away," said King George III of Blake's poetry. No wonder Quebec wants out.

Yet it's obvious when you look that these two poets are producing a body of work unique in the world, a body of work that will be of lasting interest once the fear subsides as it will in time. But for now we're waiting and wondering.

The Passe-Muraille Alternative

Brian Arnott

There are many people who believe that the year 1952 and the founding of the Stratford Shakespearean Festival mark the real beginning of the theatre in Canada. In some ways their judgment is correct. But it is only as accurate as saying that Lord Strathcona's last spike was the first official act of a unified nation. Others would—and have—argued that the CPR and the Stratford Festival both turned out ot be conglomerations of mixed blessings, qualified successes and promises unkept. The latter-day prophets who have so challenged conventional wisdom began to emerge from all walks of life in the late nineteen-sixties. They were vocal and insistent. On the transportation issue, the policies and practices of the CPR were exposed before the Canadian Transport Commission by political economists and non-political housewives. In the theatre, it was not until 1974 when the Board of Directors of the Stratford Festival announced the appointment of Englishman Robin Phillips as successor to Canadian Artistic Director Jean Gascon that public awareness of the Canadian stage assumed truly national proportions. The clamour raised by the theatre profession against Phillips made headlines across the country. Above all, it was clear that many hopes had been dashed.

On the face of it, professional discontent and disillusionment were inevitable and probably inherent in the very structure of the Stratford Festival. Also, as is so often the case, dissent from such established institutions can be charged with positive energy. The Stratford dissenters argued, in a nutshell, that the Festival had come to monopolize Canada's perception of what the theatre should be. Stratford appeared to have become the only game in a very big and sparsely populated town. It was basically British in content and sensibility. Furthermore, it was rigidly exclusive – virtually one playwright, one management, one playing place, one style, one point of view, one audience and one comparatively short season. For many, in terms of prestige at least, there simply was no alternative. But luckily by 1970 a number of like-minded young actors, directors, designers and writers were beginning to work regularly at producing a different and new repertoire for a different audience. Their principal venue was Toronto, although there were smaller groups in other cities.

The origins of this movement, which so profoundly changed the style, substance and sheer quantity of Canadian playmaking in the early nineteen-seventies, may be ascribed to the happy convergence of many circumstances, among them: the anti-establishment temper of the times, which tended to seek simpler, cheaper, traditional ways of doing just about everything; the arrival in numbers of the first acceptably trained graduating classes from university drama departments; the expression of national self-awareness in such manifestations as the Centennial celebrations and the CRTC rulings on Canadian content in the media; accessibility of LIP monies and increased funding from all levels of government; and ultimately the failure of young actors, directors, designers and playwrights to find a place for themselves in what was then a comparatively small, somewhat inflexible and significantly non-Canadian theatrical milieu. One solution was to start your own theatre: it was not only an obvious and desirable one but, more important, now it was also possible.

This new theatre movement of the early nineteen-seventies has come to be identified generally with four Toronto endeavours: Theatre Passe Muraille, Factory Theatre Lab, Tarragon Theatre and Toronto Free Theatre. Of these, Theatre Passe Muraille was the first to be established and its contribution to the development of a national theatre is unique.

Theatre Passe Muraille was founded in the spring of 1968 by actor and director Jim Garrard, who began operations in association with Rochdale College, soon to be known as the nefarious capital of counter-culture in Toronto. Garrard, a poetic and shrewd mind somewhat given to sardonic humour, was then in his late twenties. He had just returned from studying in England where he had come across a metaphor whose theatrical implications intrigued him. He had discovered a storybook character who possessed a talent for passing through walls. At one point, this character — called Le Passe Muraille — loses his power while in transit and gets stuck. This episode led Garrard to imagine that the wall in which his hero was trapped was thick, something on the order of the Great Wall of China. The combination of Le Passe Muraille's remarkable abilities and a cultural monument like the Great Wall seems to have given Garrard the idea of a theatre whose destiny and purpose was to pass through all manner of material and social barriers. Thus, when Garrard established his first theatre and drama workshops at Rochdale, he did so under the name Theatre Passe Muraille.

Rochdale College, in 1968, offered a remarkable opportunity to anyone searching for an alternative to living and learning in the conventional mode of professors, textbooks and diplomas. Rochdale was a self-governing and self-taught community of young people, which occupied its own eighteen-story building on Toronto's Bloor Street. It was an experiment in education without limits and, naturally enough, a place where anything could and might happen. Here Garrard found the attitudes and atmosphere which were conducive to the development of his theatre without limits. Ticket sales, production values and other traditional managerial concerns were made secondary to the quality and substance of the theatrical experience itself. Intensity and freedom of expression mattered more. In addition the nature of the Rochdale community demanded personal involvement; it generated a very high level of amateur enthusiasm and the search for visionary experiences was its norm. Rochdale thus became the spiritual source for values and assumptions about the theatre which were to influence the Toronto stage increasingly in the coming years. Equally important was Rochdale's practical support: a playing place two floors down in the parking garage; office space, printing and other services; meal tickets for hungry actors; and, at times, cash grants.

Theatre, like everything else at Rochdale, was substantially different from prevailing models. Theatre Passe Muraille in no way resembled Stratford, or the then recently defunct Crest or the liberal amateurs of the University Alumnae Dramatic Club or any other Toronto enterprise save perhaps some generic kinship with George Luscombe's Toronto Workshop Productions. Theatre Passe Muraille existed first for its professional members, their development and their livelihood. The concept of audience was not a traditional one, numbers of attendees being secondary to their collective or communal identity. In Theatre Passe Muraille's terminology, the audience was not so much a group that attended as it was a group that was served. While Passe Muraille's home was at Rochdale, its charter demanded that it move freely about the city. It had therefore at least two discernible audiences: one within the Rochdale building and one in the community at large. Passe Muraille's responsibility to its audiences included not just entertainment but education, both in the conventional and the Rochdalian senses of the term. Workshops were thus a high priority. Within the Rochdale building, these workshops were provided for non-professionals as well as for members of the company. At times, the workshops might become little more than "touchie-feelie" sessions. But even at the level of self-indulgence these experiences were an important part of breaking through the barriers of conventional stage behaviour. They were also the link to a new-style sensualized theatre then emergent in the US. Outside Rochdale, more subdued workshop sessions were conducted in the Ys, churches and through the school boards. For its playing places, the company was prepared to go anywhere within the Rochdale building and outside of it to high-rises, community centres and various places of work throughout the city. These outside ventures also served to provide the Passe Muraille company with badly needed income.

By the summer of 1968 the Rochdale internal workshops had spilled out into the neighbourhood where several street events were presented. In November of that year, Theatre Passe Muraille unveiled its first scripted play, Paul Foster's *Tom Paine*. This highly sensual play had been originally produced in New York under the direction of Tom O'Horgan, who has since become famous as the director of *Hair!* Although a novelty on the Toronto stage, Ron Rirrel's Passe Muraille production of the Foster play was only an hors d'oeuvre to Garrard's production of Rochelle Owens' *Futz* the following February. *Futz* had originated in the same theatre milieu as *Tom Paine*. It is a fable in which a man is in love with a pig. Simulated sex, bestiality and onstage nudity were part and parcel of the presentation. Nowhere could the contrast between the conventional middle-of-the-road play productions and this new style have been made more clear. In *Futz*, sexuality was both frank and predominant. Sensing the presence of evil and anti-social forces, the Toronto police morality squad moved quickly to close the play and lay charges against Garrard and four others.

In retrospect, it is evident that the publicity *Futz* generated did a great deal to formalize change in Toronto theatre. Furthermore, the subsequent aquittal of Garrard and the other perpetrators tended to confirm the acceptability of the new approach. Having passed through this thick wall of conventional morality, Theatre Passe Muraille found itself unexpectedly facing an open door. While it could hardly be called a popular theatre yet, Passe Muraille had become widely known in a short time and through its fame had, in a sense, been legitimized.

Because his theatre without limits was also a theatre without an accessible public playing place, Garrard had staged *Futz* in the tiny theatre adjacent on the top floor of the old library building on St. George Street – a highly unlikely venue for subversives. After *Futz* had been closed by the police, Garrard received an invitation from Jim Fiske, rector of the unorthodox Church of the Holy Trinity. The church hall at No. 11 Trinity Square was available and Passe Muraille was welcome. The $500-a-month rental was covered by the angels of Rochdale College.

No. 11 Trinity Square was essentially a large room on the order of 4000 square feet with a 25-foot ceiling. On the street end there were additional small rooms and offices on two floors. Passe Muraille's tenure of No. 11 continued from the summer of 1969 until early in 1974 when the building was demolished to make room for the Toronto Eaton Centre. During this three-and-a-half-year period, Theatre Passe Muraille changed from a theatre without limits to a theatre of mobility. The management changed too and an emphasis on Canadian subject-matter supplanted the emphasis on vivid theatrical experiences. The building at No. 11 Trinity Square figured significantly throughout, not just as a geographic centre but as an influence upon the evolving Passe Muraille style. To Jim Garrard, the building was more a geographic locale than a physical enclosure. In keeping with his original metaphor, the actors went everywhere. He might just as readily send them out to play on the roof and down into the basement as have them shrink down and use a small corner of the big room. Later, under Paul Thompson, the action centred largely on the big room and the Passe Muraille playing style adjusted very successfully in volume and energy to fill it.

In the first year at Trinity Square, Passe Muraille was run by the triumvirate of Martin Kinch, Paul Thompson and Garrard. Within two years, the cocky and elusive Thompson was running Passe Muraille by himself, Kinch had broken away to start the Toronto Free Theatre and the creation of Canadian theatre pieces had developed from a worthwhile goal to an impassioned *de rigeur.* Garrard, meanwhile, had slowly stepped back from direct involvement in Passe Muraille to help organize the FUT (Festival of Underground Theatre) Festival in the summer of 1970. Shortly thereafter, he left Passe Muraille altogether to become the *eminence grise* and a guiding sensibility of the alternative theatre.

About the time Jim Garrard left Theatre Passe Muraille, the alternative theatre movement was becoming widely identified with Canadian nationalism. While Canadian, the playmaking atmosphere was heavily charged and highly conducive to cultural self-discovery and many of its products were lauded out of all proportion to their worth even when judged by generous standards. There were no breakthroughs on an international scale to be sure. But, collectively, this work was a very important step in Canada's theatrical growth. It was a time too when there was little distinction or conflict between political awareness and aesthetic perceptions. In the years 1972-74, there was a prevailing feeling that anything remotely Canadian was either very significant or very worthy or both. While this simply was not so, there was a growing conviction that what was Canadian was not necessarily uninteresting, unworthy of examination, second-rate or unimportant to the future. As a nation we were about to take up Stanislavski's advice about loving the art in ourselves rather than ourselves in the art.

Perhaps no piece of Canadian theatre of the last decade better exemplifies this search for a collective selfhood than Theatre Passe Muraille's *The Farm Show.* As its title suggests, *The Farm Show* was a utilitarian work. Its mission was to declare proudly: this is who we are and it's good. The particular Canadians who form the protagonist "we" are a group of farmers from Southwestern Ontario. While they do not represent all Canada, they are clearly home-grown, typical and figures of the here-and-now. Passe Muraille was saying emphatically that from this moment on, Canadian playmakers would no longer need to go abroad in search of appropriate or effective subject-matter. There was drama to be found in the homeliest corners of the land, if one would only take the trouble to look for it.

The Farm Show also represented something new in play-making technique. It was theatrical found art, a rummaging for treasures in neglected places. In the summer of 1972, Paul Thompson mobilized a company of five actors and took them to the farming country near Clinton, Ontario. None save Thompson who had grown up nearby had had any measurable exposure to farming life. Each day was spent partly in visiting and working with local people and partly in a process of culling from observed reality kernels of theatrically useable material that might be refined into scenes truthfully illustrating farm life in an amusing, evocative, startling or saddening way. It was, in short, dramaturgy and performance rolled into one and practised co-operatively. It was a technique that Thompson had learned during the two years he spent with French theatrical reformer Roger Planchon in Lyons. The theatrical potential of the collective identity Planchon recognized in the French workers, Thompson saw in the Ontario farmers. The first performance of *The Farm Show* was given in the very barn where it had been developed and for the very people whose lives and identities were its subject. To this audience, every word and gesture was bursting with meaning. It was an event that contained the stuff of which great theatre is surely made.

The entertainment value of *The Farm Show* and its subsequent success in places and atmospheres remote from Clinton has probably obstructed a clear view of the play's assets and liabilities. Some observers claim that *The Farm Show* is more sociology than drama. Certainly, its form is more an assemblage than a work of the imagination. Yet, in the hands of the original cast the play did radiate an affectionate humour, an appealing vitality and a palpable honesty. It was genuinely new, fresh and likeable. Overnight, imitators of this collective creation sprouted up all over the map and, for a while, playwriting seemed threatened with redundancy. At the same time, *The Farm Show* struck a sweet chord in the public ear. Urban audiences, in particular, who were only now catching up to the back-to-the-earth movement of some years before, could feel that the decline of the family farm was their loss too. The facts of this loss were made much less bitter by the actors' obvious affection for their farming friends, who became somewhat like curios in what might have otherwise been an agit-prop event.

The Farm Show is emblematic in so many ways of the important alternatives that Theatre Passe Muraille was to choose under the leadership of Paul Thompson. As a theatrical property, *The Farm Show* was a popular success and a box-office hit. The demand the show created meant that it could be toured. Moreover, its actor-centred non-scenic presentation allowed it to be taken wherever there was an audience – community halls, livestock sales barns and formal theatre buildings. The tour's geographic focus was initially on Southwestern Ontario. Here Passe Muraille was moving into fertile theatrical territory, a small-town circuit that had been neglected since the days of Ambrose J. Small. To the people of these theatrically isolated communities *The Farm Show* was indigenous, popular theatre of a kind that had vanished with the advent of the movie house. But *The Farm Show's* availability was not just a question of subject-matter. Thompson had insured that the play's cost to local sponsors would be low enough to keep the price of admission in the $3 range. This attention to the cost factor was not incidental to Passe Muraille's artistic purposes. Thompson, who has been said to run the theatre as if it were a farm, has been acutely aware of the artistic restraints imposed by complex management and high overheads since 1967 when he spent a year as Jean Gascon's assistant at Stratford. High costs meant the loss of mobility, flexibility and access to a wide audience. Thus at Thompson's Passe Muraille, production costs were more than kept down: they were suppressed to insure that the emphasis remained where Thompson believes it belongs – squarely on the actors and the actors alone. Consequently, the proportion of the Passe Muraille annual budget that has gone to actors is probably the highest of any theatre in Canada; and the management and production costs are probably the lowest.

Thompson's sense of financial proportioning was undoubtedly sharpened during his year with Gascon at Stratford. Here he observed firsthand a lavishness that was geared more closely to public relations than to the interpretation of dramatic values. These excesses no doubt offended the sense of economy he had learned through his farming background. Thompson was also struck by the Stratford Festival's lack of concern for the cultural values of the area in which it found itself – the farmland of Southwestern Ontario. Like many others, he saw that to be successful at Stratford you had to be British. If you were a Canadian, even a Canadian who had just spent two years with Planchon, there was no way to go but out. Eventually, even Gascon himself was not spared.

Not surprisingly, then, Thompson's anti-British, anti-Stratford feelings ran high in his early Passe Muraille years. These feelings formed, shaped and guided his work. Along with many others – painters, writers, musicians – who were so moved, he began looking for Canadian heroes. He looked into Canadian history and into the part of Canada he knew best. In 1970, Thompson created a play about the Doukhobours who had lived in the Clinton area in the nineteen-thirties. It was billed as a non-sexual nudist show, perhaps the forerunner of that curious mixture of the political and the sensational that was to culminate later in *I Love You, Baby Blue* and *The Horsburgh Scandal*.

Following Doukhobours came *Free Ride,* another documentary play on the subject of hitchhiking. Then, just prior to *The Farm Show,* Thompson produced the last fully scripted play he would direct for some time, Carol Bolt's *Buffalo Jump,* on the subject of the Estevan and Regina riots in the nineteen-thirties against the R.B. Bennett government. A pattern was beginning to develop in the theme of Thompson's work: it was rural, historic, parochial and political. Technically, narrative was replaced by an episodic flow of scenes that were related only thematically; there was always an abundance of mimetic action; physical exuberance; songs, dances, parables and other editorial devices. But most significantly, there was a conscientious effort to give theatrical validity to sounds, rhythms and myths that were distinctively Canadian.

Thompson's Passe Muraille has not, however, been without its paradoxes. In a business that has traditionally been dominated by individuals either real or imagined, Passe Muraille has persisted in pursuing a co-operative playmaking formula. In all Thompson's work, there have been only two parts (Mackenzie in 1837 and Horsburgh in *The Horsburg Scandal*) that could be considered starring roles. Yet, Passe Muraille's celebration of collective heroes has been organized by a very single-minded individualist. Much of Passe Muraille's highly mobile, highly adaptable, actor-centred, low-budget style has been gained at the expense of those delights for the eye and the ear which have historically linked the theatre to an urban sensibility. Thompson's enduring concern has been for an indigenous theatre which, in his terms, means one that is spartan and direct, with values and feelings that arise from the dignity of hard physical work and rough-neck play.

The summer after *The Farm Show*, Thompson took another small group of actors to the once-prosperous and optimistic mining town of Cobalt, Ontario—a process he was to repeat the following year in the once-prosperous oil town of Petrolia. From the Cobalt experience, Passe Muraille produced *Under*

The Greywacke; and in Petrolia, it was *Oil!* Both efforts were in the mold of *The Farm Show.* Both were greeted enthusiastically by the people whose lives they reflected but neither had *The Farm Show's* popular fascination.

Passe Muraille did, however, recapture the public's interest with its next two works—*Them Donnellys* and 1837 (also known as *The Farmers' Revolt*). *Them Donnellys* touched superstitions in certains parts of Southwestern Ontario that verged on taboo. It was a sweeping epic with a large cast that generated a scale and pace of action equal to the chilling legend of the Donnelly tribe. Passe Muraille's performance was based upon the attempt merely to re-stage the supposed events. The emphasis was on action rather then interpretation. The resulting event was both theatrically powerful and the fulfilment of a playing style that had at last succeeded in adequately filling the big room at No. 11 Trinity Square. More important, however, than its theatrical forcefulness, *Them Donnellys* was demonstrably superior as drama to the James Reaney cycle of Donnelly plays that later received critical acclaim at the Tarragon Theatre. By comparison, the Reaney work under Keith Turnbull was academic, bloodless, sentimental and precious. *Them Donnellys* was followed directly by 1837, which is perhaps, when all is said and done, Passe Muraille's most complete work. Like *The Farm Show,* 1837 was a popular success. Its central story was very widely known. Moreover, it featured a Passe Muraille first, an engaging central character— William Lyon Mackenzie—whose presence glued together the two layers of history and histrionics. 1837 was also both politically significant and timely. In fact, the revolt of the farmers of 1837 had many parallels to the revolt of the artists of 1974. Its appropriateness notwithstanding, 1837 had dramatic value and durability. The more it was played the better it seemed to become. *The Farm Show,* on the other hand, had lost its charm as the actors' inspiration receded with time. Following 1837 Thompson took another group of actors into an Italian neighbourhood in downtown Toronto to create a play about the lives of new Canadians. The formula was again that of *The Farm Show* and the result, though much less popular, was a greater achievement, with far less reliance upon mimicking actual personalities and much more concentration on theatrical invention and the portrayal of typical situations. In *The Adventures of an Immigrant,* Theatre Passe Muraille explored a new and somewhat unlikely aspect of the Canadian experience. In doing so they crossed cultural barriers and enhanced and liberated the playmaking style with which they now had considerable experience. The resulting play was an Italian comedy in more ways than one.

In the fall of 1974, Passe Muraille announced its program of "Seed Shows." From his budget for that season, Thompson had set aside twelve parcels of $1000 which he was willing to offer to people who would come forward with good ideas for shows. In addition to the money, Passe Muraille would provide its aegis, publicity and space. The only credentials one needed in order to apply were conviction and enthusiasm. The idea, which was an excellent alternative to the play-readings done by other companies, was one that went back to the era of Jim Garrard, who had called these events "Side Shows." The difference between Garrard's metaphor and Thompson's is highly illustrative of the difference between these two men as theatrical producers.

The "Side Show" or "Seed Show" concept attracted a wide variety of ideas and provided opportunities for a diversity of emerging talents ranging from Codco to Hrant Alianak. One of the people to take advantage of the program in its first season was Thompson himself, who developed a show from a series of ten pictographic paintings John Boyle had done on the subject of the Riel Rebellion. The paintings were full of unusual juxtapositons (the youthful John Diefenbaker as a contemporary of the ageing Gabriel Dumont) and a company of ten actors developed in a surprisingly short time a series of thematically related scenes that explored Boyle's oblique sense of history. Typically, the show, *Canadian Heroes Series No. 1,* had the high level of physical vitality and emotional energy that had come to characterize Passe Muraille's work under Thompson.

Beyond this point, Thompson's work seemed to be at a standstill. His next production, the controversial *I Love You, Baby Blue,* captured a great deal of public attention, though none of it was due to the work's theatrical value. It was an attempt to prove that sexuality sells and, as such, it was a runaway success.

In the summer of 1975, Thompson went to Saskatchewan with his troupe of performers in an attempt to portray the prairies in the same way as they had protrayed Clinton, Cobalt and Petrolia in the preceding summers. But this time the subject was beyond their grasp, too vast and too difficult to characterize.

The next year, Thompson resurrected a sensational event from the recent history of Southwestern Ontario with *The Horsburgh Scandal.* This play, which dealt with a smalltown minister accused of encouraging promiscuity among the young people of his church, was not effective theatrically despite – or because of – the presence of Don Harron in the leading role. Harron was badly miscast; the scenario was weak; the cast was full of disparities and the visual presentation unintelligible.

Thompson's recent work (including a show about athletes in Montreal's Olympic Village; a country-bumpkin atrocity called *He Won't Come in From the Barn* and the recent *Shakespeare for Fun and Profit*) do little to indicate that he is catching his second wind.

And yet neither praise nor blame can rest with Thompson alone. Garrard's founding contribution must not be overlooked. Nor should the contributions of Anne Anglin and Miles Potter to *The Farm Show* in particular be forgotten. 1837 would be unthinkable without the work of Neil Vipond, Suzette Couture, Eric Petersen and writer Rick Salutin. David Fox and Janet Amos have figured prominently as both actors and directors. These and performers like Booth Savage have given Passe Muraille much of the dynamic force that distinguishes its work from that of so many of its contemporaries.

But ultimately, Theatre Passe Muraille has relied heavily on Thompson's energy and determination. His success lies more with the entire collection of his works than with any individual show. For whatever Passe Muraille's current powers, whether to pass through the walls of convention or to move about freely leaving a new image of Canada in the minds of its audience, it will always be known for its steadfast loyalty to the pursuit of a Canadian spirit and to a vivid theatrical expression of our national identity. According to Thompson in a recent interview taped in Stratford, "If Shakespeare were living today, he would not be working at the Festival, he would be doing what Passe Muraille is doing."

Boasting aside, he's right.

James Reaney's 'Pulsating Dance In and Out of Forms'

Stan Dragland

On 14 December, 1975 the NDWT Company ended a national tour of James Reaney's *Donnelly Trilogy* with a marathon same-day performance of the three plays: *Sticks and Stones, Handcuffs* and *The St. Nicholas Hotel, William Donnelly, Prop.* The marathon, at Bathurst Street United Church, climaxed over a decade of Reaney's research for and writing of the plays about the massacre of the Donnelly family by their neighbours in the Southwestern Ontario township of Biddulph. Posters invited the audience to share in "the agony of nine hours of theatre." Whatever the experience was for the actors it wasn't agony for me, and I believe my reaction was typical. It was one of the most enthralling experiences I've had in the theatre. I don't believe the importance of the event – if we see it as a crystallization of the whole tour and all that led up to it – has really sunk in in this country. Only a small fraction of the potential audience can have seen the plays, and since it's not a simple matter to produce a trilogy it's hard to know when it'll again be possible to attend the three plays together. All three are published now (Press Porcépic) and while the books can't entirely re-create the production, the inclusion of pictures and of Reaney's production notes and stage directions are a help. The trilogy will never be dissociated in my own mind from the NDWT production, but I don't intend to say more about production here than is helpful in a discussion of the plays as literary texts. Instead I want to talk about the results of a good deal of reading and re-reading of Reaney's work that the Donnelly plays set me off on. I believe that now is a good time for a reassessment of Reaney's accomplishment to date.

When you stand within James Reaney's art as a whole, and concentrate not so much on the distinctive world that he creates or on his recurrent themes, but rather on the forms that contain it all and the techniques that make it work, you get a different impression from what most Reaney criticism gives you. In a sense form is *the* question with Reaney. Form has been evolving; the vision has remained pretty much constant and has been a staple of Reaney criticism. Reaney has always had something to say. He has been a vigorous proselytizer for the causes of regionalism, nationalism, romance as a viable form, the iconography of the imagination, a new theatre. His art has been successful very often in proportion to the submergence of the various "causes" within it, which is a way of saying that when Reaney is at his best it's the form that carries it off.

As a mythopoeic poet Reaney has gained an undeserved reputation for being more interested in art than in life. His less careful readers have blamed his avowed interest in the criticism of Northrop Frye for what they thought was an over-systematization of experience. But the label of academic poet doesn't fit. There doesn't even seem to be a pigeonhole to put Reaney in. If you read him whole you find some unevenness, some poems or plays that don't entirely work, occasionally because of an unresolved tension between "message" and the form it takes. But everywhere you find formal experiment, a true searching out of a strong centre that takes no account of what is fashionable, even though Reaney has always been abreast of what is current in literature and the other arts in and out of Canada. You have only to look at the formal distance between *A Suit of Nettles* and *The Donnelly Trilogy* to realize that something revolutionary has happened to Reaney's art. If you look again you might see that at least in the Mome Fair eclogue of *A Suit of Nettles* thare are formal experiments that feed into the later drama. Reaney's forms and techniques are always swapping around within his work. Even his essays, his little magazine *Alphabet,* his teaching at the University of Western Ontario—everything he does has a formal aspect that flows out of and back into his art as a whole. All of Reaney's preoccupations, formal and otherwise, seen to flow into *Donnelly,* which is itself organic: everything is a part of everything else.

Looking back through Reaney from the vantage point of *Donnelly* suggests some observations:

☞ The connection with Frye has been overplayed. Reaney has been faithful to Frye's criticism, recognizing much that echoes and supports his own concerns, but he has been enough his own man to give Marshall McLuhan equal billing with Frye as a Canadian "thinker." Frye doesn't have much use for McLuhan, but Reaney does, and the connection with McLuhan has more to say about the nature of Reaney's form than does the influence of Frye.

☞ Reaney wants to do a great deal at once. Without sacrificing clarity he challenges the reader or viewer with a three-ring circus in which many things happen at once. His art is cinematic in its range, flexibility and speed. He expects a lot of his audience, but there is nothing elitist about his work. He wants us to complete it for him.

☞ The evolution of Reaney's art has been metamorphic. His experiments with form have seldom been dead ends. One thing turns into another. Forms combine with forms, poems combine and recombine in different units. There is a flowing formal continuity.

☞ Reaney aims at being comprehensive. He wants to reach us at all levels through all modes of representing reality. His centre is somewhere between myth and documentary.

☞ Reaney's art is contemporary. His work as a whole makes an open form which is of our time, though it preserves much from times past and ultimately aims at getting clear of time.

I

One of Reaney's recurring archetypal patterns is behind *Colours in the Dark*. As he describes it in the author's note, the play has "the backbone of a person growing up, leaving home, going to big cities, getting rather mixed up and then not coming home again but making home and identity come to him wherever he is." This is not original with Reaney. The story is the one Frye describes as the basis of all literature. But it's only part of what is going on in *Colours in the Dark*. The form is something else entirely: "The theatrical experience in front of you is designed to give you that mosaic-all-things-happening-at-once-galaxy-higgledy-piggledy feeling that rummaging through a playbox can give you." There is much more McLuhan than Frye in this. It sounds much like McLuhan's description of his technique, in *The Gutenberg Galaxy*, as a "mosaic or field approach" to "a mosaic of perpetually interacting forms that have undergone kaleidoscopic transformation, particularly in our time."

McLuhan challenges his readers to make their own synthesis of the mosaic of materials he presents. Reaney is not so cool or detached as McLuhan, but you often see him using a similar technique of involving the reader. One of the forces behind Reaney's little magazine *Alphabet* was his interest in contemporary literary forms. He says in the editorial to *Alphabet* 1 that "the most exciting thing about this century is the number of poems that cannot be understood unless the reader quite reorganizes his way of looking at things, or 'rouses his faculties' as Blake would say." Whatever else, *Alphabet* is an excercise in the use of the imagination, because the form it takes is a mosaic of myth and documentary out of which, as Margaret Atwood points out in a *Canadian Literature* article on the magazine, the reader is invited to make his or her own patterns. Recently Reaney has written about *Alphabet* that "perhaps it is turning into a theatre." It looks that way. *Colours in the Dark* and the Donnelly plays have the same combination of mythic and documentary material, the same juxtaposition of various forms, and the reader or viewer of the plays has again to "rouse his faculties" to make himself the place where it all comes together. The principle of involvement is explicit in Reaney's comment about the marionettes he made for *Apple Butter,* one of his plays for children. They are

☞ roughly made because I'm no Junior League seamstress, can't carve wood but also because I'm quite content with the resultant primitive effect which all the money in the world couldn't buy so far as forcing the reader to complete my work for me is concerned.

Alphabet may also have turned into the team-taught course in Canadian Literature and Culture that Reaney introduced at the University of Western Ontario. The structure of the course is certainly *Alphabet*-like. Students are encouraged to make their own connections, not only between a mixture of Canadian "classics" and unorthodox, often non-fiction, offerings (art and life), but also between the styles and opinions of several lecturers as well as supplementary slides, films and records.

Every writer searches for the form that is what he has to say. There was never much for Reaney in the form that Frye adopts, the sequential and logically structured prose argument, however beautifully done, however influential the message. Frye's matter is all there on the page. In McLuhan and Reaney the page (or, in Reaney's case, sometimes the performance) is full of gaps that, like an impressionist painting, must be bridged by the reader of viewer. Or, as Reaney describes John Hirsch's production of *Names and Nicknames* in the production notes for *Listen to the Wind,* "words, gestures, a few rhythm-band instruments create a world that turns Cinerama around and makes you the movie projector."

2

In *Alphabet* 4 Reaney prints a poem by Jack Chambers that he feels illustrates Charles Olson's idea of "composition by field" better than the poetry of most of the Canadian writers who were influenced by Olson and others of the "Black Mountain" School. The "images and meanings of the poem, as well as the mere surface format," he says,

☞ make up a beginningless, middleless and endless field of bubbling energy that reflects the current world picture. In short, if matter is a swarming cloud of electrons and landscape through air travel has become a continuous Jackson Pollock painting and Mr. Glenn Gould says that the *Goldberg Variations* begin again as soon as they end, then poetry if it wants to express this reality has quite a job ahead of it.

This vision of contemporary life sounds like the one McLuhan's technique was evolved to comprehend. Or Reaney's. Today's world is a bit of a blur in which patterns tend to get lost or appear unintelligible. One way to meet it is to work in forms that have a speed and versatility of their own, but underlying whose complexity is a shape that may be felt and discovered. Reaney works with myth, which is insoluble but also expansive, containing and redemptive, distinct from the illusory insolubility that confronts us as simply too much information, much of which we could figure out given the time and some aptitude. Long before Reaney finds his own comprehensive form that "reflects the current world picture" I can see him moving toward it.

I find the phrase "speeding it up" in Reaney's pioneering article on the nineteenth-century Canadian poet Isabella Valancy Crawford. Reaney does for Crawford's poetry what she might have done for herself had she not lived in such cultural isolation. He puts her poems into his own mutascope and turns them fast enough that the underlying pattern, her myth or vision, spins out of the dross that obscures it. Speeding it up means cutting down, simplifying, threshing, perhaps on a principle something like the one in the production notes for *Listen to the Wind,* where Reaney says "the simpler art is – the richer it is."

In a similar way, when Reaney goes looking for the backbone of Canadian poetry in "The Canadian Poet's Predicament," he comes up with a list of the passages out of an anthology that hook in him, and presents it as an epitome of the whole. Later in the essay he refines even farther, choosing one line out of each of his quotations and making a composite Canadian poem, a grain of sand containing "the native tradition." Reaney is probably more interested in encouraging others to play around with their own tradition than in establishing a definitive core, and perhaps Margaret Atwood and D.G. Jones have followed the example by reconstructing, thematically at least, the poem Canada writes. My point is that you can't turn Canadian poetry any faster than Reaney does, just as you can hardly do a quicker run-through of Canadian history or world philosophy than Reaney does in the Mome Fair eclogue of *A Suit of Nettles.* I admire the tour de force speed of Mome Fair without really getting caught up in it, but I feel something working in Mome Fair that Reaney takes quite some time to reach in his drama.

One reason the early drama doesn't work as well as the latter is that it's too slow and deliberate, at least compared with what Reaney eventually comes to in his theatre. Too slow is one way of describing some of the criticism of *The Killdeer, The Sun and the Moon, The Easter Egg* and *Three Desks:* too much exposition, too linear and chronological a progression. Reaney himself has never given up on the early plays. He admits in "Ten Years at Play" that *Listen to the Wind* marks a change in his technique that splits his drama into two periods or styles, but he maintains that his audience only needed to give in to the "primitive" technique of the early plays to enjoy them. From the time of *Listen to the Wind* on, though, there is no question of needing to bring a certain openness to the plays; they demand it. Reaney makes it easier for us to "give in" because he makes it necessary.

Reaney says in "Ten Years at Play" that from the beginning of his career in drama he wanted to "tell as strong a story as I could devise, as richly as possible." He seems to have discovered that richness requires speed, or "rapids," to find a pun on his description of the later drama in "Ten Years at Play." He says that the early plays are "constructed like rivers in voyageur journals. You go smoothly along in an apparently realistic way, and then there is this big leap" into the unusual. The later plays are "all rapids," which is to say that in them the richness Reaney aimed at has a formal dimension that includes swiftness.

The Donnelly plays move at a terrific rate, as they must to make sense and pattern of a complicated web of events spanning many years. Despite the rapid pace, *Donnelly* never blurs, and one interesting explanation is the "summary" or "epitome" scene which takes a whole play, or even the whole trilogy, and quickly passes it in review before us. Sometimes the elements of the summary are simultaneously verbal and visual, as at the opening of Act 3 of *Sticks and Stones:* "Behind [Jenny Donnelly's] narration the entire company mime groupings that go through the story backwards and forwards." Or there is the wedding dance at the Donnelly School in Act 2 of "Handcuffs," a "reprise that brings together the musical and dance themes of the whole trilogy." Whether or not there is a direct and conscious line of influence, these condensing scenes seem to relate to the trilogy rather in the way Reaney's Crawford relates to Crawford unsifted, the way Reaney's Canadian "poem" relates to our whole tradition. Or the way the whole trilogy relates to the mass of its source material.

You could call the summary scenes in *Donnelly* a kind of "shorthand," to adapt a word Reaney uses to describe the metaphorical technique he discovered while directing the first production of *Listen to the Wind,* the pivotal play that led to the later workshop drama. The early plays sometimes left an audience feeling a bit manhandled as strange things happened that they felt unprepared for by the aparently realistic technique. *Listen to the Wind* introduced a radical solution to the problem of form. It "broke with reality completely, used shorthand for everything, forced the audience to provide lighting and production and even ending...." The discovery of this shorthand was crucial to a workable combination of richness and speed. Shorthand means economy. It comes out of a strong faith in the power of the imagination to "complete" the metaphorical suggestions that Reaney's words and his actors' voices and bodies make. Reaney's basic verbal device has always been the metaphor but, as Wilfrid Watson pointed out in a review of *The Killdeer and Other Plays,* "theatre form is bilingual – the language of the actor's voice is conterpointed against the language of his body." Reaney made a great advance when he found out how to use the human body and various props metaphorically (mime, as in the Peking opera, is an influence), establishing his own conventions as he went along and inviting the audience to supply the complete images they suggest. One such visual metaphor, a wheel or carriage, Reaney sees as central to *Listen to the Wind,* and it recurs with increments and variations in *Donnelly:* "as the 'carriage' journeys with Maria to the station it should go on a journey that takes in part of the auditorium so that the boy running with the wheel 'enchants' itself into the onlookers' minds." The stage direction then slips into the comment that "in the original production this mime seemed to sum up the play. Devil

Caresfoot limps over to the 'carriage' but once 'in' it he runs like a boy." The wheel *is* a carriage. A row of chairs is a row of trees, a crossbuck suggests a train. These are metaphorical formulations. The release from realism makes just about anything possible on the stage, an almost cinematic range, not to mention that it shrinks the budget considerably – so that Stratford probably wouldn't be interested.

In *Donnelly* we have a stagecoach duel, a horse race, trains, a threshing machine–all made with human bodies and capable of "dissolving" in a minute into something else–pigs or people. When the actors *are* the props or the scenery you gain a fluidity and flexibility that the static set and unwieldy scene change work against. On the stage you see what you see, unless you are asked to imagine it.

Not only does Reaney ask his actors to be things, he also makes them multiply in another sort of economy move that also has psychological implications, two sorts of which are mentioned in separate stage directions to *Colours in the Dark*. The first explains the business of multiple characterization in this way: "The whole play is going to be like this–six characters playing many different roles–suggesting how we are many more people than just ourselves – our ancestors are we, our descendents are us, and so on like a sea." There are two sorts of visual symbol in the play which embody this formulation, two family tree pyramids (or, on the page, concrete poems), one supporting a child, one of which he supports, suggesting the privilege and the burden of containing other people and earlier times.

The other direction points at multiple characterization as a symbolic way of handling psychological complexity, the individual as a nexus of many lives. The growing boy in *Colours in the Dark* discovers "how many colours and selves he broke up into ... finding out how hostile and loving the most normal figures in one's life could be." If the continual shifting of identities in *Colours* is not confusing, and it isn't except to those who don't recognize that the convention is symbolic, it's partly because one comes to feel the containment of all the symbolic personages inside the head of the boy whose story is the backbone of the play, and also because the splits are not random. They happen in permutations of an archetypal pattern that Reaney tells us in "An Evening with Babble and Doddle" is behind *Night Blooming Cereus:* "Carl Jung's division of the human soul into four parts represented by an old woman, an old man, a young man and a young girl."

In *Donnelly* a few actors still play many characters, but the Jungian scheme is not so much in evidence because the emphasis of the story is more historically particular, and because there are in a sense two complex protagonists, a family and a community. In fact more than one community: Canada as well as Biddulph. But still, however metamorphic and fast-moving the technique, it never becomes vague because these communities tend toward polarization: Grits and Tories, Orangemen and Catholics, friends and enemies. And the neutrals, Donnellys and others, always hemmed in between the antagonistic factions. The "design images" of the trilogy help to reinforce the recurrent sense of oppositions, so that if the particular name and identity of a given character slides by at first reading or after one performance, there is little confusion about the total picture of people in opposition to one another.

3

One of the things that goes hand in hand with "speeding it up" and "shorthand" is the combination of forms and, perhaps as a outgrowth of that, ultimately a metamorphic technique. If the current world picture is an "endless field of bubbling energy," then the form that meets and matches it should probably be flowing and energetic too. When I look at Reaney's work as a whole I'm always conscious of what he calls in his introduction to *Masks of Childhood* "an organism, a pulsating dance in and out of forms." In Reaney's art, forms are tried on that nobody but Reaney *sees* as forms, forms mate with other forms, individual poems combine and recombine in different ways. This means that despite Germaine Warkentin's admirable anthologizing work, *One-Man Masque* and *Colours in the Dark* are still the best Reaney anthologies because the poems in them take the sort of place they have in Reaney's work as a whole—as parts of a large design.

From his collaboration with John Beckwith on the chamber opera *Night Blooming Cereus* Reaney dates his birth as a "craftsman with words." It may be that he learned something else from working with Beckwith. His early attempts at the libretto, he tells us in "An Evening with Babble and Doodle," were too complicated to be set to music; the words made too many claims for themselves. It sounds as if the boundary between poetry and music was too firmly fixed. "Since the librettist is supposed to write something which the music completes and extends," Reaney writes, "the lines have to be cleaned and scraped until there is nothing to stop the music flowing around them." Then a marriage of forms is possible. A librettist is something slightly different from a poet; the latter has to give a little. There is a sacrifice of the isolating ego in favour of a flexible selflessness that makes it possible to combine your words with something else – or your person. The actors in Reaney's "workshop" drama discovered what it means to contribute to something larger than self. They were asked to leave off being actors long enough to become part of a stagecoach or one of a herd of pigs – in order to turn into something else, as Reaney did writing *Night Blooming Cereus* (the poet became the librettist), as distinct forms tend to break down with Reaney in order to combine with others.

It's interesting to see what happens when music combines with poetry in "Letter Eight" of *Twelve Letters to a Small Town*. Music was important to Reaney before he met Beckwith, of course. He cites lessons in counterpoint (as well as the example of film and the three-ring circus) as instruction in making a statement on more than one level at once. Music lessons gave him the idea for the two-part invention of "Letter Eight," which uses words as notes: left and right hands separately first, then together to play a year in town. Here's a part of "Spring":

> Bud bud budling
> Bud bud budling   The spring winds up the town
> Bud bud budling
> Bud bud budling
> Buddy blossoms   The spring winds up the town
> Blossom buddies
> Budding blossoms

This is fascinating on the page, but it isn't only a page poem. It wants to lift off the page into the ear, as so much of Reaney does, and maybe it does so more readily than *Night Blooming Cereus* because it makes, or suggests, its own music. Of course one way to listen to *Night Blooming Cereus*, as Reaney puts it in "Babble and Doodle," is as "a pattern of sounds, some of them repeated many times, an arranged stream of babble...."

Patterns of sounds are what you get from time to time in *Geography Match, Names and Nicknames, Colours in the Dark* or *Donnelly,* which sometimes break into word lists chanted magically in the sound poetry, "borderblur" between words and music. In fact, by the time of *Donnelly* you have not only chanted words and phrases—sounds made with the voice—but sound effects made with sticks, stones, fiddles, a train whistle, a record-player needle – pre- or un-verbal sounds. Chants, sounds and the music of songs and dances combine to make the soundtrack weave of *Donnelly* a score that would be fascinating to hear on its own. I expect it would be intelligible, if partial, like the music for *Night Blooming Cereus.*

Reaney adds his own musical counterpoint to the poems he was asked to read on tape for the Canadian Poets series issued by the Ontario Institute for Studies in Education. Reaney's tape opens with his piano rendition of the hymn "Beulahland," which he then calls the first poem he ever heard. He hasn't been singing along, so he almost seems to be calling the tune a poem. The point is a small one, but it does point at a certain absence of creative discrimination as regards the boundary between forms, the sort of mind that would think to augment his words with music through the OISE tape.

Reaney was fiddling with the form of "the poetry reading" for OISE. He had done so earlier when he was asked to read some poems to "raise the curtain" for the hour-long *Night Blooming Cereus*. Reaney gave the audience more than its money's worth by producing a hybrid form that combines elements of the poetry reading (or anthology), the drama and the masque. *One-Man Masque* is a poetry reading, but the reading has the shape the poems are given by their arrangement, and the poems are "orchestrated" by Reaney's prose bridges, "a series of comic and macabre monologues to be performed between the poems," that come alive and stand on their own, unlike, say, Tom Wayman's dependent transitions in *Money and Rain*. Then Reaney uses the stage, or the space around the "reader" that sags during the usual reading, and fills it with visual symbols or mileposts along the two roads or journeys in life and death the poems make. Later, with more experience and some help, Reaney will liberate his static props so that they can join that "pulsating dance."

It might be worth mentioning, just to raise the tip of an iceberg, that the performance of the masque by Reaney himself, like the creation of his own marionettes for *Apple Butter*, involved erasing the line often drawn between writer and performer or production assistant: a man's life as well as his literature may be bound and limited by forms; there is a greater wholeness to be gained by living as well as writing in an interface.

One-Man Masque, "Letter Eight" of *Twelve Letters* and to some extent the OISE tape—these are not standard forms. They make a new place for themselves in the space between the forms they combine. Two or more forms are turning into something else. There is a guessing game called "Chinese

Pictures" in the first version of *The Killdeer* that suggests how Reaney likes to transpose forms, really to create a sort of metaphor identifying form with form. The game, played by Harry and Rebecca, is a riddle whose clues involve imagining the answer in different modes. "If it were/ A flower what kind of flower would it be like?" Change it into something else. Make a poem a piano piece. Give stage directions an orchestral role, as in *Night Blooming Cereus.* Expand the epigraph into almost a form of its own, like the goose alphabet of *A Suit of Nettles.* Make a metaphor without words, and not only on the stage.

Here's a visual metaphor, one of Reaney's own drawings, which illustrates "The Bicycle" in *Twelve Letters:*

Reaney's art may be connected to a thematic stable faith in the source and ultimate unity of archetypes, but the form it takes is metamorphic. That's one reason why it's so hard to get hold of Reaney – his elusiveness is sometimes taken for a lack of centre – and why it's difficult to catch the essential Reaney in anthologies.

4

If Reaney as a whole is metamorphic, *Donnelly* is quintessence of Reaney, an amazing amalgam of forms. It is so protean in its shift in and out of forms (not to mention its movement within them) that you can hardly pin down its primary debt to any mainstream of drama. Film techniques, including silent film or slapstick possibilities, offer important points of comparison. The cinema's "cast of thousands" is approximated in the technique of multiple characterization, and the shorthand with props makes almost the same range of imagery available on stage that real life offers the cinema, except that the filmmaker needs no help from the audience in creating his image; the art is less involving. The "dissolve" or "melt" from one scene or character into another has a great deal to do with the pace and fluidity of the trilogy. In fact there is enough of a cinematic nature in *Donnelly* (the long shot, the closeup, the split screen) to make that worth an article in itself. But the novel is there too in the shape of the various first-person retrospective narrators. *The St. Nicholas Hotel* is contained within the framework of Will Donnelly's account of the Donnellys' account of the Donnelly story to Rev. Donaldson, and other narrators surface from time to time in this and the other plays. The address is sometimes directly to the audience within the plays. Then there is poetry, not to be too sharply distinguished from the "poetry" of the whole, as the prose of speech is occasionally heightened into poetic statement, with accompanying changes of rhythm. There are songs — like the "John Barleycorn" of *Sticks and Stones,* which contains the whole story and is used both entire, before the play begins, and piecemeal to provide one sort of recurrent motif and to underline the action at various stages. There are dances, not simply for entertainment or variety, though they provide that. The dances arise out of the community of Biddulph, as one of the chief sources of amusement in nineteenth-century Canada, and their shapes — parallel lines or a circle — are also the forms of antagonistic opposites or unified oneness that are poles of possibility between which the community operates until what we have left is either one long line (Biddulph) menacing a dot (Donnellys), or a perversion of the circle of plenitude — a dark circle of the joined shadows of all Biddulph engulfing the Donnellys. There is puppet theatre, mime theatre, detective fiction, the classical chorus, the trial scene (actually originating in one of the many kinds of documentary material Reaney incorporates). Dramatic use is made of almost the whole Roman Catholic liturgy, which is one of the main structural features of the trilogy. We are never very far away from a mass or some other ritual feature of the Catholic faith, even if it's the Donnellys themselves who have been forced to become their own priests, their family an outcast congregation. Reaney is the author of the *Dictionary of Canadian Biography* entry on another outcast, David Willson. This amazing original, an exemplar for Reaney, was too enthusiastic in his faith for the Toronto meeting of the Society of Friends. They threw him out and he had to found his own sect, the Children of Peace.

The formal variety, the borrowing from likely and unlikely sources, makes a new form in which the most diverse elements are firmly but not obtrusively controlled. Perhaps one may nowadays safely look at this variety as something Northrop Frye accounts for in *The Anatomy of Criticism* since it has been getting clearer all the time, and more people are recognizing, that Reaney isn't tied to Frye's apron-strings. But I'll approach the idea in terms of something Reaney says about Jay Macpherson's *The Boatman*. He admires her ability to transpose (and that's something, as we've seen, Reaney often does) a theme from one key or mode to another. One way to put it, in Frye's terms, is that Macpherson turns her book through the modes of tragedy, irony, romance, comedy. This is part of the reason for Reaney's enthusiasm for the structural coherence of *The Boatman:*

☞ Not only is this poet able to arrive at a skill with a very important symbol; she also knows how to deal with a great variety of topics in a carefully modulated variety of ways. The variety of methods or ways or tones is so cleverly arranged that by the time the reader has finished the volume he has boxed the compass of the reality which poetry imitates.

Reaney gets this sort of inclusiveness too. All the modes of representing reality make their appearance in *Donnelly*. There is the gothic romance in a comically debased form in show-man Kelly's Medicine Show Black Donnellys. Irony grows throughout the trilogy in the ever-enlarging gap between the complex reality of the rights and wrongs of the total situa-tion in Biddulph, and the single blindered vision of the increasingly powerful anti-Donnelly faction. What we see happening in front of us is the creation of the vicious myth of the Black Donnellys, as a combination of racial, personal, religious and political pressures that eventually causes even normally fair-minded people to lose their powers of ordinary eyesight and common sense.

Then the trilogy is a tragedy with a comic resolution always implicit from the very beginning in the fact that it is, after all, the Donnellys who return to tell most of their story retrospec-tively. And where they return from may be seen in the words of Bridget Donnelly as she describes her end, looking out an upstairs window of the Donnelly house:

> ☞ The star came closer as they beat me with the flail that unhusks your soul: at last I could see the star close by; it was my aunt and uncle's burning house in Ontario where—and in that star James and Judith and Tom and Bridget Donnelly may be seen walking in a fiery furnace calmly and happily forever. Free at last.

Even if Frye hadn't said that the epic is the genre that contains all modes, that would seem the most comprehensive word to describe not only *Donnelly* (as Germaine Warkentin does in her introduction to the new edition of *A Suit of Nettles*), but Reaney's work as a whole.

Reaney uses a range of fictional techniques from poetic to realistic to box the compass of reality. He has always been known for his use of "strong" archetypal patterns, not so much for rooting those patterns in everday reality, as he does in

Donnelly. Actually his grip on the so-called "real" has always been stronger than has been much appreciated. For eleven years *Alphabet* placed documentary side by side with myth, as in various ways do the "Seventh Letter" ("Prose for the Past") of *Twelve Letters, Colours in the Dark* and a recent article, extending the work on media of H.A. Innis and Marshall McLuhan, called "Myths in Some Nineteenth-Century Ontario Newspapers."

Donnelly is full of documentary material that doesn't call attention to itself, being subject to the demands of the flow of the plays just like everything else. The point is that in detail we keep hearing an authentic voice of the past, often a down-to-earth emotionless voice that impassively comments on a story full of passion. George Stub calmly and smugly recites the statement of expenses for the building of a gallows while Mrs. Donnelly urgently hikes to Goderich with the petition she hopes will save her husband. During the fight in which Donnelly kills Patrick Farl an "inquest voice" breaks in with a description of the murder weapon, a "certain common handspike the value of one penny." The worth of the handspike is ironically irrelevant and revealing of the absence of perspective, the sort of mentality that undervalued the Donnellys, the "on the ground quality which materializes everything," as Reaney puts it in a stage direcion, "while with the Donnellys there is just the opposite feeling." Detail after detail like this strikes home both by being sharp and specific and judiciously placed in the flow of the play. Gradually we have built up a detailed picture of what it was like to live in nineteenth-century Biddulph. The people too, down to the minor characters, are sharply realized, and often through their language, which is one of the most amazing things about *Donnelly.* The tricks of Irish-Canadian speech are caught and contrasted with more universal, more "poetic" English on the one hand, and on the other hand burlesque stage Irish. The handling of language is remarkably sure, seeing that *Donnelly* marks the first time Reaney stepped into a world very different from his more general and usually contemporary Southwestern Ontario. One reason why it isn't necessary to "give in" to the world of the Donnellys is that it's all there in front of you in all its realistic detail.

It's one thing to identify the forms contributing to *Donnelly* and to suggest some of the ways in which the trilogy is modally and fictionally comprehensive, and it's another to get the feel of the trilogy as it makes use of forms in new ways. The triumph in *Donnelly* of Reaney's metamorphic slide from metaphor, whether visual or verbal, his "pulsating dance in and out of forms," is that it sharply registers the edges of things (scenes, characters. images) before moving on, merging them with or dissolving them into something else. If one were looking for an analogue of the spirit of Reaney's technique elsewhere in Reaney, one might find it in the poem called "Near Tobermory, Ontario" which describes the landscape in terms of a favourite organizational scheme, the four elements. Fire in this poem is light, which is seen not only as an element but as a definition of the way all the elements coexist:

But light, you're quite another thing.
   Indeterminate,
You hold them all yet let them slip
   Into themselves again.

There is also a horse (Boehme) on the philosophical merry-go-round of Mome Fair in *A Suit of Nettles* that sounds as if it bears the spirit of the technique of *Donnelly:*

... what a pretty snow white horse tattooed with stars, mountains meadows real sheep moving on them it seems & fiery comets & stars & ships in a harbour & little horses dancing in a barnyard. This horse's eyes – oh the angelic wonder of its gold red mane. Every once in a while this horse's colour completely changes. People shy away then I can tell you! Storms break out in the tattooed skies and a fiery fire burns in the eyes. However it bubbles over – a light comes into his eyes and the world changes back again.

I would have said that the Heraclitean horse, whose "whole form keeps flowy-changing," is also illustrative, but in Reaney you *can* "sit in the same saddle twice," because a principle of recurrence controls the flow.

If *The Anatomy of Criticism* stands somewhere behind the form of *Donnelly* (well back), so does the galaxy or mosaic technique of Marshall McLuhan, but McLuhan as he might be interpreted by the metamorphic animated film techniques of Norman McLaren.

One reason why *Donnelly* seems to me to concentrate all of Reaney formally is that he appears to have brought to the story all that he feels about life and literature, all his writing experience, and sunk those things into the play, so that one not only feels less of Frye here than elsewhere but, for all the intricacy of the mechanism, less of Reaney too. I think that is because the form does so much. Almost everywhere in Reaney we find, sometimes quite schematically, the conflict between the anti-poetic materialists and the "identifiers" or the unthinking advocates of progress versus the believers in subtler laws of existence or educators of the soul as opposed to educators for practical life. These conflicts, or variations on the one conflict, are present in *Donnelly*. They help to define the Donnellys not only as individualists but as people who go against the common assumptions of their time and place. The conflict is central, but set in such a wealth of flowing event and detail that it doesn't stick out, as it does in the post-Donnelly *Baldoon,* a delightful play which nevertheless reverts to the lobbying for the value of love and the imagination that Reaney has been engaged on for so long.

Donnelly is an extremely complicated machine, all of whose working parts are open to view. There is the feeling Jay Macpherson got from *Listen to the Wind* of "creation before one's eyes," perhaps even stronger in *Donnelly* because the dramatic metaphor ("how do we make this play" within the play?) is assumed. There is nothing hidden from us by a backstage. The actors sit on the stage and move into their parts when they are needed. Or they make sound effects using everyday objects that are also visible. All this contributes to the audience's co-creation of the trilogy and is worth a great many Reaney exhortations to go out and make our own plays, to rouse our slumbering imaginations.

Donnelly is an anti-environment, to use McLuhan's phrase, the form of which is familiar to us, whether we recognize it or not, from our experience of speeded up, bewildering modern life. But the metamorphic form is bent to the expression of permanent values and has a shape (one of those values) that may be discovered, that controls its constituent parts centripetally, while the fragments of contemporary existence seem centreless, centrifugal. But perhaps the best way to deal with the form of the trilogy is to say that it is *of* the Donnellys. It has their wit, their verve, their openness, their sense of humour; it has their wings, their refusal to kneel. Even the simultaneity of the story seems to be of the Donnellys. The murder happens in *Sticks and Stones* and happens again and again one way or another throughout the trilogy, and there are other ways of dislocating and contracting time that only the Donnellys, of all the protagonists, seem connected to. For one thing the ghost selves of the Donnellys know all the story, having "passed into source." But sometimes we see them even in the "present" of the play living fleetingly in the future, as when Mrs. Donnelly predicts that she will come once more to Father Connally's church after she has decided, in this life, never to enter it again, or when she dimly senses the presence of her "deep down dead leaf self" in Act 2 of *Sticks and Stones*. The trilogy has the largeness of spirit extending even to the breaking of the barriers of time, of the Donnellys themselves. Which is to say that you may tell almost all there is to tell about *Donnelly* by talking about form. That isn't inevitably true of other individual Reaney works, but it seems true of Reaney read whole as, to adapt some words of Irving Layton, his forms "swap, bandy, swerve" in an overall shape that is both open-ended and under control.

The Human Elements:
Margaret Laurence's Fiction

George Woodcock

There are times when an unconsidered remark can set one on paths of speculation that a cautiously critical approach would warn one to avoid. Recently I was involved with a friend and fellow-writer in one of those interminable and inconclusive discussions of writing in Canada which always, despite Northrop Frye's warnings of the perils of evaluation, tend to become mired in arguments about comparative quality. Having let myself be led into this profitless morass, I had argued – I thought very convincingly – that more good poetry is being written in Canada today than in Britain (certainly) or in the United States (probably). Then my friend turned to the discussion of fiction. Did we – could we – have a Canadian equivalent to Tolstoy? My answer, impulsive and without any previous thought, was immediate: Yes, Margaret Laurence! My friend treated it – and so did I after a moment's thought – as one of those rash and immoderate statements one makes when cornered in a discussion. Afterwards, as I thought about what Tolstoy means to me and compared it with what Margaret Laurence means to me, I was tempted to elevate my answer from the status of a rash impulse to that of a flash of insight.

Consider the proposition, not in the terms of literary

gigantism in which we are traditionally inclined to approach writers like Tolstoy, Homer, Shakespeare and Balzac, but rather (leaving posterity the futile task of comparing statures) in such terms as a writer's relevance to his time and place, the versatility of his perception, the breadth of his understanding, the imaginative power with which he personifies and gives symbolic form to the collective life he interprets and in which he takes part.

There are some writers whose visions, true as they may be, are so intensely personal, or so restricted in terms of locality or class, that whatever national flavour they may exhibit seems an undesired accident of language, of place and time of birth. But there are others who seize on such accidents to inspire and strengthen their work, and these are the writers who one can say (since greatness has become so abused a word) have a largeness of scope and vision and even of verbal texture, combined with a vigour of opinion and even prejudice, that expands their work, without destroying any of its personal intensity, into an expression of what the German romantics called the *Zeitgeist,* though I would widen the context to include place as well as period, for what is extraordinary about most such writers is their grasp of space as well as of time, so that what they recreate and preserve for us in their writing is a view of the land, and of the way people grow out of it, so convincing that no historian conveys to us—for example—the physical texture as well as the spirit of archaic Greece so vigorously—even after two and a half millenia—as Homer does in the *Odyssey.* The same applies to most cultures; each of them has its truth-telling bard, though the genres the bards use may differ. For the true feeling of late mediaeval England, where the sense of man as an individual emerges vigorously out of a tribal past, we go to the poet Chaucer; no writer provides a truer reflection of Spain in his century (or in any other country) than Miguel de Cervantes, despite the churrigueresque frame in which he enclosed the luminous mirror of Don Quixote's dreams and adventures; Thomas Mayhew, with his descriptions of the lives of the early nineteenth-century London poor, was a superb early sociologist, yet we now read his book mostly as an historic curiosity, and it is through the fictionalizing genius of Dickens that the world Mayhew described really comes alive for us.

In this company of writers who fulfil one of the great functions of art—the preservation of lost times and worlds in such a way that outsiders can imaginatively apprehend them—Tolstoy and Margaret Laurence both belong, and there is a particular closeness between them in the fact that each is seeking to find a way of dealing with a land of exceptional vastness, and also to reconcile a sense of history in a time of rapid change (for revolution or not, Tolstoy's world was in rapid transformation as the steppes were opened to cultivation and the Trans-Siberian moved eastward to complement the westward thrust of the CPR) with a passionate sense of the importance of personal experiences and particular destinies. The special quality in such writers lies not so much in the grand physical and temporal scope of their vision (for Spengler and Arnold Toynbee have had a similarly grand scope to their vision of history without being imaginative artists by any definition) as in the fact that their characters are as impressive as their settings, and their best revelations are achieved not—as Tolstoy ineffectually attempted to do in the expendable theoretical sections of *War and Peace*—by the explicit statements of historic themes, but rather by the vivid, concrete yet symbolic presentation of crucial points of insight in individual lives, such as Levin's drinking of water from a rusty tin cup in the splendid mowing scene of *Anna Karenina,* or the moment in Margaret Laurence's *The Stone Angel* when the despised minister, Mr. Troy, sings the first verse of the Doxology to Hagar Shipley during her last days in hospital and, on hearing the line, "Come ye before him and rejoice," she suddenly realizes, "I must always, always, have wanted that—simply to rejoice. How is it I never could?" and then reaches the crucial and almost life-giving insight that

"Pride was my wilderness, and the demon that led me there was fear." It is an intensely personal recognition for Hagar Shipley; at the same time one can generalize it into a description of the state of mind of a whole generation of English-speaking Canadians.

Tolstoy in his special way projected the vision of a whole generation of Russians. It was a time of exceptional literary flowering, and there were other writers who in terms of sheer artistry could certainly compete with him. Turgenev, for example, who better than any other projected the mental agonies of nineteenth-century educated Russian youth, the essential humanity of Russian serfs, the sight and smell of Russian woodlands on a hunter's morning; Dostoevsky, master of existential agony and of the psychopathology of a land history seems to have doomed to recurrent tyrannies; Chekhov, unparalleled recorder of the nuances of perception and disillusionment in an intelligentsia that already, years before the cataclysm of 1917, feels itself doomed: all are splendid, as are the autobiographical chroniclers like Herzen and Aksakov and Kropotkin, but all, in comparison with Tolstoy, are incomplete, because none possesses his panoramic sense of a great steppeland haunted by history; none, for all their skills in exploring individual psyches, was so well able to present man as a member of a living community; none understood with such agony the ambiguous role of the artist in a world of moral crisis; none was so ready to sacrifice his own art once he felt its relevance was exhausted or its function superseded.

I think we can say similar things in comparing other contemporary Canadian writers with Margaret Laurence, and this I am sure is why her image has dominated our last decade in the same way as, according to W.H. New, the fifties in Canada were dominated by the image of Hugh MacLennan, with his rather bald and elementry insistence on such basic Canadian themes as the recognition of national imperatives and the perils of the everlasting duality he christened "the two solitudes."

There are some ways in which MacLennan too resembles Tolstoy, mainly in his less successful didactic aspect. And Margaret Laurence is not entirely without didacticism (indeed, I have never yet read a major novelist who quite dispensed with it). But, though she recognizes quite as strongly as MacLennan the national imperative and the forces that militate against its survival, she is much less inclined to subordinate the aesthetic to the homiletic in her writing. The nation and its perils are there, to be described, to be seen, to be felt, but not to be argued about, at least in fiction.

Margaret Laurence positively resembles Tolstoy in possessing the panoramic sense of space and history, developed to a degree no Canadian fiction writer can rival (though Al Purdy may perhaps in verse). She understands the importance of our newly recognized myths that bind us collectively, and to order and direct her sense of community she has created her own imaginary and exemplary town of Manawaka, so near to and so far from her native Manitoba town of Neepawa that she can say, "in raging against our injustices, our stupidities, I do so *as family,* as I did, and still do, in writing about those aspects of my town which I hated and which are always in some ways aspects of myself." She has always felt a salutary doubt about the completeness of the writer's role as a seer, and she expresses it in the final pages of *The Diviners,* where novelist Morag's old friend Royland tells her that he has lost the power of finding water.

> At least Royland knew he had been a true diviner. There were the wells, proof positive. Water. Real wet water. There to be felt and tasted. Morag's magic tricks were of a different order. She would never know whether they actually worked or not, or to what extent. That wasn't given to her to know. In a sense, it did not matter. The necessary doing of the thing—that mattered.

And, like Tolstoy, she seems to have the will to declare a vein of creation exhausted, for she has publicly declared that *The Diviners* is her last work of fiction, and in the years since its publication in 1974 she has shown no sign of revoking her resolution.

Such resolutions, proclaimed by a writer in her early fifties, seem made to be broken, and one can do no more than hope that Margaret Laurence's creativity will again clamour for fictional expression. At the same time, as I shall show in the latter part of this essay, there is a completeness about the Manawaka novels as they stand, not only in terms of a common setting and interlocking characters who share the same origin, but also thematically in the dominant archetypal structure.

Margaret Laurence's writing, almost entirely prose, falls into two categories, the fiction and the discursive non-fiction which is partly autobiographical and partly critical. The fiction, in turn, falls into two groups, that concerning Africa— *This Side Jordan* (1960) and the stories collected in *The Tomorrow Tamer* (1963)—and the Manawaka books, consisting of the four novels, *The Stone Angel* (1964), *A Jest of God* (1966), *The Fire Dwellers* (1969) and *The Diviners* (1974), as well as the cycle of stories, *A Bird in the House* (1970), that is really a kind of episodic novel in which time flows through the narrator's childhood, while the setting is constant and there is a recurring group of main characters.

Except for the final novel, *The Diviners,* whose present is set in the kind of rural Ontario background where Margaret Laurence was actually writing the book, all of her fiction is set in distant places which she experiences in memory and imagination. Africa is the setting of fiction written in Vancouver. The Manitoba where Laurence spent her childhood is the terrain of novels and stories written in Vancouver, in England and in rural Ontario. Physical and temporal distance become, in the Canadian novels at least, essential to the very structure of the works, which are patterned not only on the recovery of time through memory but also on the kind of consciousness of horizontal space that is peculiar to countries of vast open distances and dramatically varying landscapes, like Canada and Russia.

Significantly, there is one area of Margaret Laurence's past about which she has written no fiction. This is the two years she spent in Somaliland, the years described in that superb travel book–perhaps the best ever written by a Canadian–*The Prophet's Camel Bell* (1963). I am not proposing to discuss in any detail Margaret Laurence's non-fiction, which is subject enough for a separate essay, but there are two aspects of her writing about Somaliland which are eminently relevant to a discussion of her fiction. Both *The Prophet's Camel Bell* and her earlier book – in fact her first book – on Somali oral literature entitled *A Tree for Poverty* (1954) deal among other things with the necessary distance from which she had to observe and then to enter, with a surprising depth of empathy, a culture that was to her intensely strange in its manner of dealing with a precarious existence in one of the world's most barren terrains. She experienced that existence imaginatively through observing – often in the harsh directness of drought and famine conditions – the lives of the Somalis, and also through the special entry into their minds that was provided by the tales and poems which she painstakingly learnt to translate during her years there as the wife of a dam-building engineer. From this complexity of contacts she gained at least two things useful to a writer.

First, there was the ability to enter from a steadily narrowing distance into a world she wished to explore imaginatively, and this she did repeatedly in later years even when she was dealing with a society – that of the Manitoba small towns – which had once been her own. The other lesson is perhaps best explained in a statement of her own about Somali oral literature.

The most deep and far-reaching realism is combined with an acceptance of life that is neither cynical nor despairing.

The Somali sees what elements make up his life, and does not seek to deny them, harsh as they may be.

In a way this statement—which one might certainly apply to the Canadian novels Margaret Laurence was to write in later years – is amplified in *The Prophet's Camel Bell*, which is not merely about the experience of being "a stranger in a strange land," but also about the parallel experience of self-discovery that can be set off by the shock of immersion in a totally strange culture.

As Margaret Laurence says on the first page of *The Prophet's Camel Bell*, "the strangest glimpses you may have of any creature in the distant lands will be those you catch of yourself." And, indeed, for those who are concerned to understand the mind that later wrote the Manawaka novels, not the least important aspect of *The Prophet's Camel Bell* is the process of the narrator recognizing and shedding one by one the pretences in and through which she has lived until she begins to see more clearly than ever before not only the reality of the land and life around her, but also the reality of her own self. And self-knowledge, accompanied as it inevitably is by a measure of self-distancing examination of one's past existence, is as priceless a gift to the novelist as it is to the philosopher. If Somaliland did not provide Margaret Laurence with material that she found appropriate for developing into a novel, it awakened in an extraordinary way the kinds of perception that she needed to become a novelist, the awareness of one's self as well as one's experience as a source the imagination can tap.

That West Africa rather than Somaliland should have provided the content of Margaret Laurence's earliest fiction can doubtless be explained in two ways. First, the people of the Gold Coast, as it was then called, were more accessible than the Somalis in terms of everyday personal intercourse, partly because in the cities at least they had absorbed a great deal of the colonizing culture, partly because many of them spoke

English or at least pidgin, and partly because their resentment against the imperialists, though it was doubtless no less intense than that of the Somalis, was not so frequently expressed in terms of open hatred. For these reasons relations between the whites and the subject peoples were at the same time freer and more ambiguous on the Gold Coast than in Somaliland. The Somalis were so certain of the rectitude and sufficiency of their Moslem culture that liberation for them meant merely re-establishing their own Islamic world, free of infidels and infidel influences. The West Africans, on the other hand, found their way toward freedom at least in part through accepting alien political concepts; those most adept at combining new political techniques with old loyalties would eventually rise to the surface as the political leaders of liberated Africa.

The understanding of such truths meant a further stage in Margaret Laurence's journey through self-knowledge and knowledge of the world to the possession of her imaginative kingdom. It is significant that she wrote her fiction on West Africa, as she wrote *The Prophet's Camel Bell,* not on the spot, but after she had left the continent of Africa in the fair certainty of never returning. She herself has told how she found that the diaries she had kept in Somaliland provided only the notes for the narrative that emerged eventually as *The Prophet's Camel Bell,* and we can assume the same to be true of *This Side Jordan* and the stories that make up *The Tomorrow Tamer.* In these books she was writing of the Gold Coast hovering on the edge of the independence that would transform it into the modern state of Ghana. She wrote partly out of experience and partly out of imagination, and it is important to observe, in view of the widespread assumption that the Manawaka novels are successful because they are autobiographical, that the more imaginative passages in the African writings – those most detached from their creator's own life – are the more convincing.

On the one side in *This Side Jordan,* the side of experience, are the group of whites who represent a British export firm on the Gold Coast. Somaliland taught Margaret Laurence the danger of distinguishing between white imperialists and other whites in a colonial situation, and her representatives of empire are now shown with a mingling of irony and compassion. These are not the grand imperial comquerors; they are, like most of the British who went out to the colonies, men who were or have become unfitted for life at home, so that they live a double exile, like so many of Margaret Laurence's characters even in her Canadian novels. They range from the tragic figures like Bedford Cunningham, a perfect gentleman whose time has passed and left him stranded in a morass of alcoholic failure, through Jonny Kestoe, the feral product of a London Irish slum who is willing to betray any of his associates for the sake of promotion, to Kestoe's incongruous wife Miranda, a well-meaning romantic whose attempt to create a bridge of understanding to the African world involves the black schoolmaster, Nathaniel Amegbe, in humiliation and dishonour.

The world of the Cunninghams and the Kestoes is the one to which Margaret Laurence belonged in Africa, the one she knew from day-do-day participation. If Miranda Kestoe is clearly not a self-portrait, she shares the enthusiasms of her creator's first years in West Africa, for, as she remarks in a recollective essay in *Heart of a Stranger,* Laurence then "wore my militant liberalism like a heart on my sleeve" and was anxious to impress educated Africans "not only with my sympathy with African independence but also my keen appreciation of various branches of African culture...." Before she left the continent, Margaret Laurence had grown out of these naïve manifestations of her interest in African culture, and the understanding that followed enabled her to enter imaginatively into the lives of the African characters, poised as they are between three worlds (the pagan past, the colonial and missionized present and the independent future) and to express the tensions that are most dramatically expressed in the inner conflicts and shifting emotions of Nathaniel Amegbe, son of one of the great pagan drummers, but also a practising Christian and a believer in the struggle for freedom, shocked by the despair of his English-educated journalist friend, Victor Edesui, who prophesies with bitter accuracy the generations of oppression by their own people that political liberation will bring to Africans. This aspect of *This Side Jordan* reveals a splendid power of intuitive insight into minds shaped by another culture, and it lives with brilliant authenticity in the mind. But in delineating the white world that parallels the changing native world of the Gold Coast, Margaret Laurence is trapped in the literalisms of insufficiently reconstructed recollection, from which she tries unsuccessfully to escape by grotesque devices like the series of macabre coincidences (a mother who bleeds to death in his presence from self-abortion, an African bush girl who bleeds when he lies with her, Miranda's redeeming blood when he witnesses her childbirth) that seem vainly directed toward turning Johnny Kestoe from the rather ordinary cad he is into a figure of melodramatic interest.

The stories in *The Tomorrow Tamer*, which appear to have been written after *This Side Jordan*, are Margaret Laurence's best early work, more unified in form and texture than *This Side Jordan*, and written with a vivid sense of physical detail that memorably recreates the African setting. As she does later on, in the stories that comprise *A Bird in the House*, Laurence seems to be using these short fictions as experimental devices to work out techniques she will later elaborate into larger forms, for many of the pieces, like "The Rain Child" and "The Drummer of All the World" are really life stories, small novellas, in which a character mingles recollection with self-analysis in the attempt to discover the meaning of his life and – of course – of his world. For no Laurence character is a solipsistic island; Violet Nedden, the missionary teacher in "The Rain Child," reveals herself through her concern for the children who are misfits in both her school and the African community around it (the actual "rain child" is an African girl marred by British education who finds her own people's way of life as incomprehensible as she finds their language), and the tragedy of the narrator in "The Drummer of All the World" is that Africa, which is his real home where he was born and brought up – a missionary's child – among native children, has changed so much that there is no longer a place for him, and the very friends of his boyhood reject him as an alien. *The Tomorrow Tamer* is, indeed, largely a book about aliens and alienation. Some of the whites, like the characters I have just discussed, have come in their varying ways to think of Africa as their own land, and when they return to the country called home they face an exile that will end only in death. Others mingle hope with resignation; they have to because Africa is the end of their roads. In "The Perfumed Sea," perhaps the most beautiful and the most convincingly triumphant story of all, the hairdresser Mr. Archipelago declares gaily, "I am flotsam," and indeed he and his woman partner Doree, with their mysteriously innocuous pasts, had wandered far over the earth before they encountered each other in a small West African coast town where the wives of the imperialists provide their living. Independence comes, the white women go, but Mr. Archipelago and Doree are of neither the imperial nor the native world; they are even curiously detached from each other, though they share the same business and the same sea-sprayed house (their main common pleasure is the guessing of exotic perfumes at nightly sniffing sessions). Yet there is a loyalty which their predicament calls forth; they adapt, as they have always adapted in the past, winning a black in place of a white clientele, and so these two pieces of human flotsam evade submersion; survival is their victory. Thus, by concentrating on the theme of the "stranger in a strange land" that first occurred to her in the bewilderment of her early days in Somaliland, Margaret Laurence breaks away from the cliché situation of racial confrontation, and by evading the excessively documentary portrayal of the white world abroad that marred *This Side Jordan,* she anticipates some of the major thematical and structural concerns of her later Canadian novels, involved as they are with the complexities of a multicultural society.

Particularly important in such a context is the curious kind of reconciliation at a subterranean level that takes place in the stories of *The Tomorrow Tamer* between the apparently opposing worlds of imperialists and Africans. The most powerful stories about Africans in this volume, those which resonate most persistently in the mind and in memory, are also of alienation and of types of exile. In "The Voices of Adama" a bush boy whose kin has been wiped out by an epidemic finds a new village and a new tribe in a regimental military band where he serves as drummer, and when he finds after five years that he is being led through a misunderstanding to accept at the time of independence a discharge that will take him away from the band and his beloved drum, he kills the white bandmaster. A black officer, Major Appiah, visits Adamo in his cell, and the bush boy's only fear is that he will lose the regiment that has become his family and his village. "I will stay?" he asks.

> Major Appiah had come to tell Adamo when the trial would be held, perhaps even to prepare the man for the inevitability of the verdict. But he said none of these things, for he saw now that they could make no difference at all. Adamo would discover soon enough what ritual would be required for restitution. Perhaps even that made little difference. It was not death that Adamo feared.
>
> "Yes," Major Appiah said, and as he spoke he became aware of a crippling sense of weariness, as though an accumulation of centuries had been foisted upon himself, to deal with somehow. "You can stay, Adamo. You can stay as long as you live!"
>
> He turned away abruptly, and his boots drummed on the concrete corridor. He could bear anything, he felt, except the look of relief in Adamo's eyes.

Adamo's survival is possible only through the group; he is in everything a tribal man, and alienation from the tribe is for him death. But even in the African world, there were those who do not belong in the tribe, whom some flaw like genius or dwarfdom has placed outside tribal normality. In *The Tomorrow Tamer* this condition is exemplified in one of Laurence's most haunting stories, "Godman's Master." Moses Adu, a westernized African travelling in the bush, unwillingly rescues a midget who has been kept in a stuffy box by a village juju man to serve as an oracle. He takes Godman, the midget, into the city, and there he finds his life dominated by this strange small being who defines their roles with so much assurance.

"You are my priest," Godman said. "What else?"

Moses could not speak. Godman's priest, the soul-master, he who owned a man. Had Godman only moved from the simple bondage of the amber-eyed Faru to another bondage? And as for Moses himself – what became of a deliverer who had led with such assurance out of the old and obvious night, only to falter into a subtler darkness, where new-carved idols bore the known face, his own? Horrified, Moses wondered how much he had come to depend on Godman's praise.

Eventually, plagued by conscience yet anxious for liberation from this dwarfish incubus, Moses expels Godman, and only sees him months afterward when he has become a berobed fortune-teller in an African freak show. They meet, and the talk is of fulfilling one's role in existence.

Godman shrugged.

"I have known the worst and the worst and the worst," he said, "and yet I live. I fear and fear, and yet I live."

"No man," Moses said gently, "can do otherwise."

The same could be said by and of a great many of Margaret Laurence's later characters in novels and stories set in Canada, and this, I think, underlines the importance of the stories in *The Tomorrow Tamer* as representing an advance in Laurence's awareness of the human condition. In a changing world the colonists and the colonized alike feel the pangs of exile and alienation.

Yet once we have recognized the generalities of the human condition, it is in the particular instances that we can best express them, and above all in the particular contexts we most intimately know, and this, I suggest, is why, after writing the remarkable group of stories on Africa collected in *The Tomorrow Tamer,* Margaret Laurence abandoned the continent as a setting for her fiction, and turned back to her own country and—since Canada is a confederation of regions rather than a nation in the ordinarily accepted sense—to her own *patria chica* of the Manitoba small towns, from which her protagonists emerge to challenge and eventually to endure the world. They fear and fear, like Godman, and yet they live.

It seems appropriate to go on now to *A Bird in the House,* rather than to the Canadian novels that preceded it in terms of publication, not only because it also is a volume of stories, though of a much more intimately united kind then *The Tomorrow Tamer,* but also because its stories were written during the same period as the first three novels about Manawaka people, *The Stone Angel, A Jest of God* and *The Fire Dwellers.* Furthermore, as Margaret Laurence tells us, *A Bird in the House* is "the only semi-autobiographical fiction I have ever written."

To admit even to semi-autobiography is quite extraordinary in an age when novelists are inclined to react with some ferocity to the suggestion that they are really writing about themselves. In the broad sense, of course, they write about no-one but themselves; as Flaubert said on the legendary occasion, "La Bovary? C'est moi!" But there are differences between the process of shucking off various personae to isolate the germs of one's more important characters which—being relatively uninventive beings—most novelists do in most of their novels, and the much more direct process of reshaping one's own crucial life experiences, usually undergone in adolescence, until they acquire the plausibility of good fiction, as D.H. Lawrence did in *Sons and Lovers* and Joyce in *Portrait of the Artist.* It needs, I think, a high degree of cultural certainty to write this type of openly autobiographical fiction, and this may explain why in Canada, where colonial inhibitions weighed heavily upon writers until very recently, it has rarely been done successfully, just as there have been few really satisfactory Canadian autobiographies. In this context Margaret Laurence's own remarks in *Heart of a Stranger* about *A Bird in the House* are very interesting, because they illuminate not only the extent to which autobiographical elements can dominate writing against the writer's will and largely without her being aware of it, but also suggest where the real-life town of Neepawa, where Laurence was born and brought up, merges into what she has fervently maintained to be the fictional microcosm of Manawaka.

In the essay entitled "A Place to Stand On," discussing the differences between those real and imagined towns, Laurence says of the people who founded prairie towns, "They were, in the end, great survivors, and for that I love and value them." She then goes on:

> The final exploration of this aspect of my background came when I wrote—over the past six or seven years—*A Bird in the House,* a number of short stories set in Manawaka and based upon my childhood and my childhood family, the only semi-autobiographical ficion I have ever written. I did not realize until I had finished the final story in the series how much all these stories are dominated by the figure of my maternal grandfather, who came of Irish Protestant stock. Perhaps it was through writing these stories that I finally came to see my grandfather not only as the repressive authoritarian figure from my childhood, but also as a boy who had to leave school in Ontario when he was about twelve, after his father's death, and who as a young man went to Manitoba by sternwheeler and walked the miles from Winnipeg to Portage la Prairie, where he settled for

some years before moving to Neepawa. He was a very hard man in many ways, but he had had a very hard life. I don't think I knew any of this, really knew it, until I had finished those stories. I don't think I ever knew, either, until that moment how much I owed to him. One sentence, near the end of the final story, may show what I mean. "I had feared and fought the old man, yet he proclaimed himself in my veins."

And this account of recognition is followed by a statement that must be given weight—but not too much weight—in considering Margaret Laurence's major novels.

My writing, then, has been my own attempt to come to terms with the past. I see this process as the gradual one of freeing oneself from the stultifying aspect of the past, while at the same time beginning to see its true value—which, in the case of my own people (by which I mean the total community, not just my particular family), was a determination to survive against whatever odds.

More than any other of Margaret Laurence's Canadian books, *A Bird in the House* can be seen as fulfilling this role of exorcising "the stultifying aspect of the past," and this makes one wonder how far the writing of these stories, during the period when the first three Manawaka novels were written, in fact served as a kind of valve by which the feelings of personal identification and agony that surged up while writing about a prairie setting were deflected from the major works in progress.

Yet these stories and the novels that are contemporary to them are really very closely linked. *A Bird in the House,* after all, is about childhood and adolescence in Manawaka, and this is an experience which the central figures of all the novels share with Vanessa McLeod, as they share the departure from the town that she makes by the end of the book. Places like Manawaka are made to escape from and then to remember the rest of one's life. But while the others mostly remember (for only Rachel Cameron in *A Jest of God* lived out the novel's present in Manawaka) through the screen of an intensely lived present (Hagar's dying days, Stacey's marital agony, Morag's writer's travails), Vanessa recollects, in almost total and unimpeded clarity, how the child's eye saw and the child's mind interpreted that vanished past. It is a clear and primal vision of Manawaka we are given, undistorted by later passions: a vision of the family – or rather the conjoined families of the Irish Connors and the Scottish McLeods—as the microcosm in which all the passions life will later magnify are seen in miniature, in the frustrations and conflicts Vanessa perceives with a knowing child's foresight will become her lot in womanhood. On the rare occasions when the narrator's present does intrude it is to give a symbolic emphasis to something a child has seen clearly but without full understanding, as in the story dealing with the death of Vanessa's grandmother and with her grandfather's inarticualte grief. It is entitled "The Mask of the Bear," and it ends:

> Many years later, when Manawaka was far away from me, in miles and in time, I saw one day in a museum the Bear Mask of the Haida Indians. It was a weird mask. The features were ugly and yet powerful. The mouth was turned down in an expression of sullen rage. The eyes were empty caverns, revealing nothing. Yet as I looked, they seemed to draw my eyes toward them, until I imagined I could see somewhere within that darkness a look that I knew, a lurking bewilderment. I remembered then that in the days before it became a museum piece, the mask had concealed a man.

Margaret Laurence's four Manawaka novels are concerned with the masks of women (and let us remember that the original meaning of *persona* was a mask used by a player) and the bewildered real selves who peer through them at the world. In every case there is a concealed self, sustained by a flow of memory and inner monologue; there is a mask that is kept perpetually in place when one moves in the world; and the world is a place where beings masked by prejudice and fear confront each other and occasionally drop their masks and come together in freedom and love. Just as *A Bird in the House* has settings and characters in common with the novels, so it had this double pattern of love and conflict, exemplified in the heart of Vanessa's own life by the conflict between the Scots and the Orange traditions and in the village by the conflict between the vastly contrasting lifestyles of the puritan pioneers like Grandfather Connor and the métis family of the Tonnerres, descendents of one of Gabriel Dumont's rebel followers in 1885, who live in a peripheral shack hamlet as a perpetual reproach to Manawaka's conscience until at last, in *The Diviners,* the conflict is resolved in the person of Pique, daughter of Scottish Morag Gunn and Jules Tonnerre, and the symbol of freedom through reconciliation.

But, despite the constant shading off between *A Bird in the House* and the four novels, the latter stand on their own, and are far more closely linked than they first appear. There is of course the common physical ambience of Manawaka, with its single main street and its prominent cemetery and "nuisance grounds." There is the fact that individuals and clans, like the Camerons and the McLeods and the Kazlicks and the Tonnerres and the Pearls, move in and out of the novels from beginning to end. There is the fact that every central figure is a woman, which establishes a line of biological and cultural consistency through all the emotional and attitudinal differences between four such variant personalities as Hagar Shipley, Rachel Cameron, Stacey McAindra and Morag Gunn. There is also the underlying sense that, in a much less overt and didactic way than MacLennan in the preceding generation, Margaret Laurence is presenting a paradigm of the Canadian condition, with the relationships of its characters exemplifying the divisions and distrusts and imperfect understandings and frustrated longings that make up the collective psyche of Canada:

Anglo-Celts and later immigrants opposed and meeting only for mutual injury in *A Jest of God,* alien and native strains finding their painful way together in *The Diviners,* the puritan cult of duty and the call of desire conflicting to make the hell of *The Fire Dwellers,* and in *The Stone Angel* the rigidities of invading mercantilism opposed to the vanishing liberties of the frontier in the marriage of Hagar Currie and Bram Shipley. All the characteristics and complexities of our national existence, at least so far as it has been lived west of the Shield, can be found in these four novels by those who search diligently enough, and this comprehensiveness would be alone sufficient to justify regarding Margaret Laurence as the kind of national novelist I have suggested she is.

When we come to look at what unites the books – even though they are not a formal tetralogy – on a deeper and more mythical level, we encounter a pattern which may not be deliberate, but which nevertheless seems clear and definite. There are four novels, and though the group is discontinuous in terms of a single uniting plot line, and is not closed off by any dramatic life-event, Margaret Laurence has declared very firmly that *The Diviners* is the last novel she will be writing. Such a statement made by a writer of great creative and mental vigour before her fiftieth year can hardly be accepted as final in terms of Margaret Laurence's life-work, but it can be taken as meaning that a phase of writing has ended, and that *The Diviners* does in fact complete a task Margaret Laurence had in mind when she began to draw Manawaka out of her imagination and to give its people life in the pages of her books. It completes a pattern.

The pattern that I see uniting the four books and defining them as a group is an ancient one. It is that embraced in antique and mediaeval science and medicine, and deriving from the 2500-year-old theory of Empedocles that the universe is composed of four elements: earth, air, fire and water. Out of this conception emerged the theory – more familiar in literary history – of the four humours that dominate human physiology and temperament. The humour corresponding to earth is the choleric; to air, the phlegmatic; to fire, the sanguine; and to water, the melancholic. Scientifically both theories may be primitive and disproved; in terms of myth they are as potent as the zodiac, and the links between the humours and the elements run through poetry and drama and fiction from classical antiquity down to the present. When we look at Margaret Laurence's four Canadian novels in the light of such archaic concepts of the nature of matter and of man, the correspondences between her works and the ancient patterning are far too close to be dismissed.

If the very title of *The Fire Dwellers* were not itself loaded with intent, the novel's double epigraphs should be sufficient to establish the dominance of the element of fire. The first is a verse of Carl Sandburg, in which he speaks of himself as "I who have fiddled in a world of fire, / I who have done so many stunts not worth doing," and the second is the old rhyme, "Ladybird, ladybird, / Fly away home;/ Your house is on fire, / Your children are gone." When we read the extraordinary monologue of middle-aged Stacey McAindra (born Stacey Cameron, the Manawaka undertaker's daughter), remembering her prairie past, trying to live in her precariously middle-class Vancouver present, keeping the peace with and between four children and longing for sexual adventures before it is too late, it is not only the fire of a world threatened with holocaust that we like Stacey are aware of, but also the inferno of unsatisfied urges in Stacey herself, the fires of a sanguine and insatiable temperament.

For Stacey's sister, Rachel Cameron, spinster schoolteacher who has never escaped from Manawaka, her mother's impositions or her own fears, the epigraph of her novel—*The Jest of God* —is equally meaningful, for it begins with the lines: "The wind blows high, the wind blows high, / The snow comes falling from the sky...." Wind is air and air is undoubtedly Rachel's element; air the insubstantial, the wavering, that which flees from fire yet feeds it, as in the crucial incident when unwillingly, at a Pentecostal meeting, she is touched by the flames and realizes to her horror that she has been speaking with tongues. Rachel, according to her humour, is essentially phlegmatic in behaviour, for apathy as well as timidity prevents her from making decisions forced upon her. Earth is as hostile to her as fire; when Steve Kazlick lays her on the ground and takes her middle-aged virginity, the result is not the pregnancy she half hopes for and half fears, but a benign tumour that is earth's mockery manifested as flesh. When her wind shifts and she leaves for her new life in Vancouver (a change of air as it were), it is air that seems to convey her, for the image she conceives of the bus carrying her and her mother away at last from Manawaka is not that of a creature running on the earth, but of one that "flies along, smooth and confident as a great owl through the darkness." Air is her element and in the end her liberation.

The stone angel, whose likeness Margaret Laurence first saw in a cemetery in Genoa on her way to Somaliland (and recorded in *The Prophet's Camel Bell*) is, of course, hewn out of the earth and blind as creatures that live in earth, and as such is an appropriate symbol for Hagar Shipley, that choleric earth-mother who inhabits *The Stone Angel*. That novel – of all Margaret Laurence's works – shows the closest and most sensual awareness of the earth's surface, of its creatures (animal or vegetable), of its colours and textures and smells. Hagar is an intensely visual but even more an intensely tactile person, concerned with what is evident to the sense of feeling, whether it is sex remembered vividly and in detail into her nineties, or the texture of a dress she wears in old age. Even her own body she often apprehends in terms of earthly mass, as one feels sculptors apprehend the forms within the mineral masses with which they work. Earth in the sense of land is also important to her, and it is as much to lie on his farm as to be ploughed sexually by him that she marries the socially impossible Bram Shipley; she resents the fact that Bram wastes his land on grazing horses instead of tilling it and making it productive.

Even as she approaches death, and her life tends to be more and more dominated by the immaterial world of memory, the memories themselves tend to be defined and initiated by the material objects from the past that surround her and which she treasures.

To this passion for the earth and its emanations in sensation and memory, Hagar adds the choler of her appropriate humour. It is in anger that she confronts her equally choleric father and insists on marrying Bram. It is in anger that she finally leaves Bram, in anger that she drives her son John from the house and thus indirectly causes his death, in anger that she flees to her illusory seaside refuge in the deserted canning factory when her other son Marvin proposes to put her in an old people's home. Every one of the people she encounters is seen through the dark screen of her choler, and it is only in the end that the black bile seems to leave her and she is able to regret the absence of rejoicing in her life and to accept the blessings of another element, though even when she takes the water as her life ebbs, she still reacts, as she had always done, with choler. The nurse offers her the water:

> "Here. Here you are. Can you?"
> "Of course. What do you think I am? What do you take me for? Here, give it to me. Oh, for mercy's sake let me hold it myself!"
> I only defeat myself by not accepting her. I know this—I know it very well. But I can't help it—it's my nature. I'll drink from this glass, or spill it, just as I choose. I'll not countenance anyone else's holding it for me. And yet—if she were in my place, I'd think her daft, and push her hands away, certain I could hold it for her better.
> I wrest from her the glass, full of water to be had for the taking. I hold it in my own hands. There. There.
> And then—

We are what we are, Margaret Laurence seems to be suggesting in *The Stone Angel,* and the nature we have been given will shape our lives and remain with us to the end. Hagar is always Hagar, with all that name signifies in terms of bondage, whether she changes her surname from Currie to Shipley, and no matter how she may change her status, and at most – as a grace – she can have a vision of what she might have been if she had not been herself.

But Hagar is the most bound by her nature of all Margaret Laurence's heroines, and bound perhaps because of the special opacity of the earth-born. Stacey, like fire, is more mutable, able to shift from the blaze of self-destructive passion to the glow of love and loyalty, and Rachel finds that those of air compounded can soar and escape as well as wavering before more solid natures.

It is water that provides the governing symbol for *The Diviners,* and here again the pattern of the elements and humours continues. Water begins the novel – the image of the river beside which the novelist Morag Gunn lives and writes and remembers, and which appears to run both ways, as our inner life does.

The river flowed both ways. The current moved from north to south, but the wind usually came from the south, ripling the bronze-green water in the opposite direction. This apparently impossible contradiction, made apparent and possible, still fascinated Morag, even after the years of river-watching.

Note that in this effect, right at the beginning of *The Diviners,* there are two elements involved, air and water; this, as we shall see, is a novel largely concerned with the elements reconciled.

Yet water is dominant. The river is not merely a pleasant foreground for Morag's dwelling; it is also a thoroughfare by which her neighbours visit her, and among these neighbours there is one – old Royland – who acts almost the same role in the novel as the old magician archetype in Jungian mythology, and who – like Merlin but in another way – is a diviner.

Royland divines water, and for Morag the link between his

occupation and hers is obvious. She also is a diviner, plunging into the depths (the very word we use is significant) of human hearts, though what she emerges with may not be so tangible as Royland's findings.

The imagery linking writing with water is of course copious. The poets draw their inspiration from the fountains of the muses on Mount Helicon and from the Castalian spring sacred to Apollo at Delphi. We think of their poetry as flowing, we talk of streams of consciousness in fiction. We associate Shakespeare with a river—the Avon—he left in youth, and see a special significance in the association of Coleridge and Wordsworth with the Lakes; we find a particular appropriateness in Shelley's death by drowning (the drowned poet has even become a dominant image in Canadian verse), while we remember with a special poignancy that Keats described himself as "one whose name was writ in water." So the associations of Morag's craft with the river that flows before her door is traditionally appropriate. (But note another mingling of the elements here; it is water welling from the earth—as Royland detects water held by the earth—that inspires the poets.)

But there is more than finding water to the matter of divination so far as this novel is concerned. It has occurred earlier in Morag's life, long before she met Royland, when the town scavenger of Manawaka, Christie Logan, would "tell the garbage" to determine the fortunes of the community's inhabitants. And Christie Logan, who took the orphan Morag into his house after her father and mother died in her infancy, is the one who introduces Morag to her Celtic past, to her ancestor Piper Gunn who led his people on to the ships for the long voyage (water again) to their homes in Lord Selkirk's Red River Settlement, and to the Celtic self that lives within her, the Dark Celt she sees as Morag Dhu, the self whose melancholy is the humour related to the element of water. (Morag is related to the Welsh name Morgan, and Morgan-le-Fay was an enchantress skilled in divination.)

Morag herself is indeed like water, secretive but enduring in her passions, able to flow round life's obstacles, caught in the endless stream of creation and full of the pools of intuition from which inspiration can be fished by the assiduous angler. The very end of *The Diviners* is undefined, incomplete, flowing on into the unknown, according to the very nature of water. Morag walks beside the river, sees it seeming to flow both ways, and detects here a paradox within her own consciousness. *"Look ahead into the past, and back into the future, until the silence."* And then she goes on to the questioning:

> How far could anyone see into the river? Not far. Near shore, in the shallows, the water was clear, and there were the clean and broken clamshells of creatures now dead, and the wavering of the underwater weed-forests, and the flicker of small live fishes, and the undulating lines of gold as the sand ripples received the sun. Only slightly further out, the water deepened and kept its life from sight.

Yet there is another aspect of *The Diviners* to be noticed, for the truth of divining, as of writing and other arts, lies in perceiving relationships, and it is an essential aspect of the ancient doctrines of elements and humours that they cannot exist apart. A healthy world is the elements combined in balance, a healthy being is the humours combined in balance, though destiny lays a bias on each of us by giving us special natures, and we spend our lives trying to achieve the equilibrium. Hagar is only aware of the need for equilibrium at the very end, but Stacey and Rachel progress in their own ways of understanding, and Morag, because of her calling and largely despite herself, comes nearest to an understanding of the pattern.

She is helped toward it by her relationship with three men. One is the professor of English she marries, Brooke Skelton, as much a being of air as Rachel was, fearful of the hostage he will give to earth if he and Morag have a child, and concerned in literature with the aspects that least relate it to the surface of the earth, the real passions of women and men. Dan McRaith, Morag's painter lover in London, is a man of earth, tied to the Cromarty seashore whose forms and colours dominate his paintings and faithful in his fashion to the woman who has been his wife since girlhood and has borne his children. The human eyes in his paintings look through the forms of rock or fossil and the emotions they express are of distance and dispossession, of spirit by earth imprisoned.

Fire is in Jules Tonnerre, Morag's first lover and the father of her child Pique. Apart from the fact that his very name is linked to the natural fire of lightning, he is associated in memory with the fire that destroyed his demoralized sister Piquette and her children and which Morag witnesses as reporter for the Manawaka newspaper. Her daughter by Jules is given Piquette's name, perpetuating the link with fire; at the same time, like fire and water, Morag and Jules can never live together, though it is tempting to think of her inspirations as the emanations of their contact, springing like gilded mists from a river touched by the sun's fires.

If in these personal ways Morag's life suggests the reconciliations existence demands between and within human beings, in a more general way *The Diviners* presents the summation of Margaret Laurence's vision of her land and her culture, and places her firmly in the humanistic and quasi-realistic tradition of the true novel as distinct from the other forms of fiction (parable, fable, satire, fantasy, romance) in which the creation of plausible worlds of the mind is not essential. Manawaka is a plausible world, not because we recognize in it Canada – or English-speaking Canada at least – in microcosm. Margaret Laurence has contended that our mental roots do not go very far back, which is why the Manitoba small towns of her parents and grandparents are for her the essential rooting place of a Canadian consciousness, yet she recognizes that such a consciousness can be expanded by experience, and Morag, like all Laurence's leading characters, departs for Vancouver (and lives in Ontario, which the others do not); she also makes the pilgrimage to the ancestral home of Scotland, and her reaction is much like that which Laurence expresses for herself in *Heart of a Stranger:*

> I care about the ancestral past very much, but in a kind of mythical way. The ancestors, in the end, become everyone's ancestors. But the history that one can feel personally encompasses only a very few generations.

Yet the myth remains essential, the Scottish myth of exile from the Highlands to Christie and Morag, the métis myth of Riel and Dumont to Jules Tonnerre. But myths gain their greatest significance when writers give them the forms in which they influence the collective mind of a people and continue to stir the collective memories. The Trojan war would have been an unremembered tribal skirmish without Homer's epics, which turned it into a myth that has inspired men for millenia. Macbeth would have been a virtually forgotten figure in the history of a bleak northern country if Shakespeare had not made him into a grand exemplum of nervous villainy; and what Spaniards would think of their past if Cervantes had not written *Don Quixote* or the French of theirs if Balzac had not existed it is now impossible to say. The novels of Manawaka, I suggest, are already playing this mythical role for Canadians. Hugh MacLennan was also a mythographer, presenting us to ourselves on the heroic level; it is amazing how many of his leading characters are sketched as Homeric giants (soldiers, boxers, crusaders, politicians, all larger than life). But the need for that kind of self-image has been fulfilled. Now we need to see ourselves as we are, as those who survive in that ordinary life where the only heroism is to endure — often to endure one's own given nature—and, to the best of one's ability, to create. It is thus that Margaret has shown us to ourselves in these superb novels, which are the best of our place and generation.

Notes on Contributors

Brian Arnott is a theatre designer and consultant in Toronto. He has reviewed Toronto theatre extensively for *That's Show Business* under the pseudonym Brian Boru. He is the author of *Towards a New Theatre: Edward Gordon Craig and Hamlet*.

Stan Dragland teaches English and Canadian literature at the University of Western Ontario and writes extensively for Canadian little magazines. He is one of the editors of *Applegarth's Follies*.

Trained in music at the University of Toronto and in English Literature at Cambridge, Peter Harcourt has taught film at the British Film Institute, Hornsey College of Art, Queen's and York. He is the author of *Six European Directors* and *Movies and Mythologies*.

Naim Kattan is Head of the writing section of the Canada Council. His most recent book is *Farewell, Babylon*.

David McFadden is a well known and prolific poet. Formerly a proofreader and reporter for the Hamilton *Spectator,* he now

162

writes full time. His most recent collection of poems is *On the Road Again.*

Kathy Mezei teaches English literature at Simon Fraser University. She is the translator of Anne Hébert's *The Silent Rooms.*

Bronwen Wallace recently returned to Kingston from Windsor. She has published poetry in many American and Canadian magazines. She has been active in the women's movement, as counsellor at a women's centre and a teacher of natural childbirth.

George Woodcock recently retired as editor of *Canadian Literature,* a magazine that he founded and edited for eighteen years. He has written widely on a great variety of topics, including anarchism, Canadian federalism and India. His most recent book of poems is *Notes on Visitations.*